ABOUT THE AUTHOR

Polarbear AKA Steven Camden is a writer from Birmingham who moved to London for a girl.

His debut young adult novel 'TAPE' was published worldwide in January 2014 by HarperCollins to rave reviews and his second novel, 'IT'S ABOUT LOVE', published in June 2015, was Book of the Month for The Guardian. His third novel 'NOBODY REAL' was recently published in May 2018.

His collection of spoken word stories 'EVERYTHING ALL AT ONCE' was published by Macmillan in July 2018.

Under his performance name Polarbear, he is one of the most respected spoken word artists in the UK and has performed his work from California to Kuala Lumpur, via Glastonbury, Latitude, Camden Crawl and pretty much every festival going. He came to prominence as part of Apples & Snakes Exposed tour 2007 and has since written and performed three feature length theatre pieces; If I Cover My Nose You Can't See Me (Birmingham REP), RETURN (BAC and mac) and Old Me (Roundhouse) on national and international tours.

Twitter: @homeofpolar
Instagram: @homeofpolar
https://homeofpolar.squarespace.com/

ABOUT VERVE POETRY PRESS

Verve Poetry Press is a new press focussing initially on meeting a local need in Birmingham - a need for the vibrant poetry scene here in Brum to find a way to present itself to the poetry world via publication. Co-founded by Stuart Bartholomew and Amerah Saleh, it will be publishing poets this year from all corners of the city - poets that represent the city's varied and energetic qualities and will communicate its many poetic stories.

As well as publishing wonderful collections from poets with local links, such as Casey Bailey, Nafeesa Hamid, Leon Priestnall, Rupinder Kaur and Polarbear, we will also work with other poets who have close connections to our sister festival, Verve. Our Experimental Pamphlet Series, our poetry show collection from Matt Abbott and our anthology with Lunar Poetry Podcasts all fall on this side of our activity.

Like the festival, we will strive to think about poetry in inclusive ways and embrace the multiplicity of approaches towards this glorious art.

So watch this space. Verve Poetry Press has arrived!

www.vervepoetrypress.com
@VervePoetryPres
mail@vervepoetrypress.com

Polarbear
The Second City Trilogy

VERVE
POETRY PRESS
BIRMINGHAM

PUBLISHED BY VERVE POETRY PRESS
Birmingham, West Midlands, UK
https://vervepoetrypress.com
mail@vervepoetrypress.com

All rights reserved
© 2018 Steven Camden

The right of Steven Camden to be identified as author if this work has been asserted in accordance with section 77 of the Copyright, Designs and Patents Act 1988.

No part of this work may be reproduced, stored or transmitted in any form or by any means, graphic, electronic, recorded or mechanical, without the prior written permission of the publisher.

FIRST PUBLISHED NOV 2018

Printed and bound in the UK
by TJ International, Padstow

ISBN: 978-1-912565-12-2

Cover art by Tristan Vanger

For
Teodosia & Glensford
who sung a strength I still dance to.

The Second City Trilogy

If I Cover My Nose You Can't See Me

—

Return

—

Old Me

These pieces are made for the mouth.
They come to life when spoken.

If I Cover My Nose You Can't See Me

(2007)

produced by
Birmingham REP and Apples & Snakes
script development and dramaturgy by Yael Shavit
design by Gabriella Gerdelics
live visuals by Goonism

Part One

Friday.
My eyes look tired in this light that's not real
strange how it can feel like time's passing but not moving
day to day
like sitting on a train in the station, waiting to pull away, waving
through the window to the kid on the train adjacent
and in the split second that stasis is broken, you look at each other's
faces unsure as to whose train's still and whose is in motion.

I could say it's funny how things turn out
I was only supposed to be here two weeks
now it's been four years and
one third of my monthly income is taken by the education I didn't use
to get me this job I don't want to pay off the degree I earned to
answer phones.

I'm a broken record.

Two charity shop shirts, one battered hand-me-down tie and tired
brown cords rotate on a five out of seven day basis fooling no one
so I come in here
Four or five times a day knowing that even if any of my co-workers
have noticed in between scribbling notes on post-its
they wouldn't say
Not to my face anyway

Or maybe they know
that I'm a 27-year-old man stuck on a loop that every day involves me playacting taking a shit

I used to hold it in when I was young. On the football pitch I'd offer to go in goal and stand stern-faced, legs crossed until the urge passed. We'd lose a goal or two but everyone knew I was no keeper. On the days when we rode our bikes I'd pretend I thought I had a puncture and role-play checking for air leaking, the whole time tensing my abdominal muscles, straining against nature so I wouldn't have to go home and miss something

Now here I am
Staff Toilets. Hiding from my day.

I know what he'd say. He'd say what he always says,
Just quit, leave. Stick two fingers up at the whole place and breeze. And part of me agrees, believe me, I must have at least seventeen daydreams between nine and five where I walk out of this trap and grab the rest of my life
Then it's like
another side of my mind kicks in
The side that prides itself on realist deterministic thick skin
It says,
This is what people do. A job is where you have to go, not what you need to do. Now get your head down and make your money cos think about it, if every day was sunny there'd be no need for the summer.

Like Harrison Ford in Bladerunner, you don't realise you're a robot til you spend some time with the others
Our 3rd floor open plan office is an open hand promise that slowly closes in on the day and the staff are like some kind of United Colours of Benetton advert for decay
Like Jane, a 38 year old girl prone to panic, emotional damage and an over-excitement for salad,
- Look, this one's got croutons in!
Has it?
Or Mavis, a middle-aged single mom whose one prized possession is a photo of her as a contestant on Jim Davidson's Big Break playing with Steve Davis.
When I told her I thought Jim Davidson was racist she just went quiet and pulled one of those faces intended to remind me exactly what my place is.
There's Dean, nineteen and born to work in an office. He drinks expensive expresso coffees and smells of lemon fabric softener. On a Monday morning he's always talking in his broad brummie accent about some girl who could have been an actress that he met Friday night. About how he banged her over the washing machine or nailed her on the stairs. When I ask him why it all sounds so aggressive he just stares, then carries on with his pornographic story.

Most days they all just fucking bore me.
I feel like I'm supposed to be somewhere else.

Thank god for Malcolm.

Malcolm Fox, the Leo Sayer-haired wearer of paisley shirts and never a pair of socks. He always knocks on my desk like it's a door when he comes over even though I can see him coming. I call him 'The Encyclopaedia Comedian'
cos he knows stuff and he's funny.
The in jokes we share save me and random film and book references, and often conflicting yet respected musical preferences are exchanged daily.
He's a maverick.
A choice I think he made as the only way to handle it, cos in this monotonous lifestyle that's lifeless, maybe it takes electric shock hair and bemused co-worker stares for that piece of mind that's priceless.
Malcolm always says,
- If things don't alter, they'll stay as they are, word to the wise.
He never mentions a family, but there are echoes in his eyes.
I've told Jess about him. About how he can name the year, director and studio for every film Marlon Brando ever made, or his ability to break down any life situation with a football analogy using a famous game played or how his ties are made from the same material as curtains, or how when he calls me son it feels like I've always known him.
I don't mention any of the other staff, on those nights when I get back late and I go straight to the bath where I know she lies naked and warm under a blanket of bubbles, her face glowing by tea light and the room is a cave and I sit on the floor with one arm reaching over and the tiny flame crackles as my hand makes a hole in the foam, like I'm ice fishing in a dream, and through that portal I can see a snap shot of her body, darker under water

my girl
submerged and my sole purpose is to make her laugh at least once before she asks me to pass her a towel.
I don't say anything else about work. Once I leave it disappears until morning.
Like mist. A grey daydream, that takes time and gives money.
Instead, I listen to Jess, about the bitching and political mess that is a primary school staffroom. About a boy that just joined from another school who the other staff refused to allow in their groups and how it boils her blood and
as her mouth moves
I notice the grooves above her lip and how the wet edge of her hair sticks to the left side of her neck, curling round into the bath water like vine on a
peanut butter-coloured tree reaching for the river.
She loves her job and though I've never known that feeling, I know it's nice to be around.
Just quit.
His voice lives in my pillow.
And as Jess sleeps next to me spread out like a starfish I lie straight on my edge and explain my life.
The rent needs to be made and I say I hate it but it pays me and the truth is that I'm safe and that safety's made me lazy.
He's always said it.
Safe David.
Just to get me mad, and it does, cos things that are true sometimes do that.

I know what I am and
that's the worst part
I'm Bruce Wayne in a Robin suit. Doing what I've gotta do
So when he tells me to quit, I wanna hit him
and hug him at the same time
Ever since I've known him we've been like that.
I remember that first day when he parked his Raleigh 'Mongoose' on the bike rack, he had the look in his eyes of a kid ready to fight that said if you bite me, I'm a bite back.
And he did. Pretty much straight away. Playing football that break he wouldn't take any kicks from any of the others, even the ones from the year above us and he clearly loved pissing them off. I liked that.
Before he came they all used to kick the shit out of me for not passing, but after that first day when he worked his way around nearly ten kids then when the biggest one kicked him he put his fist in the kid's face then passed to me in the space and I scored the tap-in while everyone ran to see the damage, my kicking never happened.
In that fifteen-minutes things changed.
By then Maradona was playing for Napoli and after school we happily played one-on-one skill marathons emulating our hero til the sky went deep red.
I remember in PE one time after we'd worked a sublime one-two, ending in me flicking the ball up, and him following through with a bicycle kick like Roberto Baggio the teacher had a go at us.
- As long as I make the rules, you'll never play for this school.
- Why?
- Because there's no 'I' in team.

Riley looked him straight in his eye and said,
- Team doesn't have an 'I', but I've got two and I can see your team's shit.

One weeks detention later we were best friends.

It was about that same time that I first saw Jess. One afternoon in a classroom we'd shared for half a year, she just appeared, and that was that

I remember I forgot to breathe as in one second everything I'd previously thought about girls was taken to one side and told,
- Oi, You've got to leave.

I didn't really understand it, cos it hadn't been planned, but as the fingers on her left hand stroked strands of pinecone-coloured hair behind her right ear in what looked like slow motion, my river reached the ocean.

In that second things changed.

I remember getting home that day and going straight to the kitchen where I knew my granddad would be working on dinner, all day soup with spinners and within a minute of being home I'd pronounced my eternal love for Jessica Brown. After granddad told me to slow down I tried to explain what had happened, about how the pink and white chequered pattern on her dress had left me flattened and how when she bit her bottom lip with the bottom bit of her top two teeth to think, nothing else mattered.

We became three. Jess, Riley and me.
Through climbing trees and ten o'clock sunsets
Through 3 Feet High and Rising and doing the running man
to Mantronix at afternoon school discos wearing dungarees

and acid suits. Through those spots on your forehead with the worst ever timing, and an awkward perfect first kiss in the park pressed against each other like movie stars and the burn of first shaves and exams and college and a car trip to Cornwall. Through fumbling in a sleeping bag by torchlight with Portishead playing on a tape running out of batteries and the taste of Jack Daniels and not really knowing what we were doing and the feeling of being inside her staying long after she fell asleep.

Through arguments about leaving home to study and following her to a new city and floating through a degree and Riley deciding he was a weed dealer and getting stoned and fights and throwing stones up at windows at four in the morning. To moving back home and talking about getting our own place and the look on her face when I told her I'd been offered a job and that we had a deposit and finding a flat in the same building on the same floor in fact across the hall from the one that I grew up in and her saying it was fate and starting her teacher training and me riding the excitement blind to the fact that the whole time my life was stuck somewhere between fast forward and rewind.

To here.

A place with no windows.

A place where I've actually timed the space between the pre-programmed flush of the urinals. 32 seconds.

A place where my boss thinks flirting means pinching my arse and double entendres.

A place where people get possessive over stationary.

A place where nobody knows who I am.

I get the same bus every weekday morning. The 140,
which comes somewhere between seven forty and seven forty five. A carriage carrying the same characters on a well-worn path to boring lives. If I close my eyes I can see them. A grey cast of people with a firm disbelief in the term carpe diem.
Tired suited businessmen with dark eyes. Long let go dreams of high flying in penthouses with exotic dark wives. The heavy drinking livers of red broken blood vesselled faces leave traces of vain bottle bottom escape attempts from dark lives.
Seventeen-year-old factory floor Friday night dreamers. All tracksuit bottoms, proud mom packed lunches and shadowed upper lips. Two months into forty year careers already rehearsed actions of carbon copy days, page three pinned under developing muscled arms.
That woman. The one who smells of old fashioned soap and pride. Knocked out of her stride into a new routine since last year when her husband died.
Her arse is one and a half seats wide and the one time I tried to sit next to her I had to kind of perch on one cheek and by the time we reached town I was numb in the backside.
There's usually a couple of students talking their mix of coursework and useless verbal abuse and that used to be me. But these days I usually choose to switch into a half-awake state until my autopilot moves me off the bus to where I'm supposed to be.
This morning though, there was someone else, someone I couldn't help watching.
A boy.
I'm guessing nine, or maybe ten, but a young ten.

Wearing a dark blue parka like you used to get, with the bright orange lining and the hood you can zip right up and pretend it's the periscope of a submarine, a fake fur frame on the world.

His stays zipped down as his young lips mouth words I can't quite work out from where I sit near the back. He seems to be reading over whatever he wrote down into a small notepad that came from his battered rucksack.

He blends in and yet stands out

down near the front amongst the usual suspects of the bus crowd and for most of the journey he doesn't do much but look down.

Dark brown hair cropped close might curl given half a chance and after the occasional glance up when his pale face looks like he came up with an idea he makes notes with what looks like one of those small pencils you can steal from Ikea in his notepad.

I can't see his eyes clearly and I'm sure at one point he nearly caught me staring, so I looked down, and those scuffed brown shoes that he's wearing

have definitely seen a football.

Part Two

Now school's started

It's harder to get into town and back before register.

So today I faked a note saying I've been sent to the doctors.

It's pretty easy, you just need to get last year's report that mom signed and find some paper thin enough so when you hold it up to the light you can see through it.

Then what you do is trace the signature onto the thin paper then get some better letter paper, put it underneath and go over the signature again in pen and this time press hard. Now when you lift off the thin paper the signature impression from you pressing has stayed on the better paper and you just have to go over it again carefully in black, cos mom doesn't use blue and put the report back cos leaving traces is slack and that's the tricky bit done.

The rest is just making sure you get the loop in the 'd' and the 'l' as well as the 's' with no top and it's really important you don't stop once you've started, just keep the pen on the paper, like mom does when she writes fast.

I've done it plenty times in the past and no one's ever asked any questions.

Graphology. That's what it's called, and if the round bit of your 'b' is balled too tight or your 'k' looks wonky or your words lean to the right they can tell if you might be angry or upset or a murderer.

I keep practising in my pad.

Practise makes perfect.

There's always a shopping list on the fridge to copy and as long as you don't get sloppy and try to explain too much you're fine. Just the facts,

Dear Miss Burly,

I would be grateful if you would allow David to leave half an hour early for lunch today so he can make his doctors appointment. He'll be back in time for afternoon class. Many thanks.

Yours sincerely, P.M. Gardener.

That's it, and it worked just like every other time I've used it, which is why I'm so stupid, cos I'm already late and if this bus doesn't come I'm gonna miss him anyway.

Things I know so far.

1. He lives across the hall in flat 15 with a lady who must be his girl-friend.
2. He doesn't suspect anything
3. His girlfriend has dark shiny hair and wears a scarf that goes round her neck twice.
(I've followed her too. She works in our school over in the infants)
4. He works in an office in town and wears the same brown trousers every day.
5. He catches the bus at 7:40 in the morning and 5:00 in the afternoon with an hour-long lunch break between one and two. (I've followed him at lunchtime twice this week already).

It's not my fault I'm late.
It was the new kid. And I know it sounds stupid cos before school

today I never even knew him, but now I feel like I've always known him.

At break this morning, playing football like always, he just showed up. In our school colours with dark side parted hair looking grown up. Usually when new kids start the older ones throw stuff, especially Danny Jones, but today they didn't and without saying anything he was playing with us. We were a man down so we got him and straight away I spotted he was alright.

He had a wicked touch and could do what he wanted with his left or right. His dribbling was ace, and the look on his face said he shouldn't be messed with and the best bit was, he kept passing to me.

Now I'm good. I'm not quite big enough, but I can play though. I've got a pretty good right foot and I sometimes wish it was my left like Diego but I can't complain though. The others call me greedy, which is really them admitting they need me cos there's always at least one genius in all the best sides.

This morning we were like Maradona and Van Basten running round going past em like they weren't even there and that goal where he flicked the ball in the air and I came round the back and whacked it top corner, was awesome.

We even Hi-5ed, even though we know Hi-5's are lame, but this one wasn't the same. We really meant it and after I got chopped down and scraped my hand on the ground he found a spot in the wall and bent it round up and down and left the goalie dumbfounded. Brilliant. Danny Jones nearly had a fit, and for a second I thought he was gonna hit me for cheering but as he came near me, the new kid moved in between us and frowned and in front of everyone, Danny Jones backed down. I couldn't believe it.

That's why I'm late. It wasn't planned, and I think I've still got a little bit of grit in my hand.

Imagine a grain of sand.
Now imagine every grain of sand on a beach.
Now imagine all the beaches you know.
Now imagine all the beaches in the world.
In our universe there are one million stars for every grain of sand on every beach on the planet.
I don't know how many that is, but I know it's a lot.
We went to a beach once but there was no sand. Just pebbles, and rocks and when you lifted up the rocks little rusty coloured jumping insects tried to escape.
Jenny didn't like the beach or the jumping insects or the grey sea. I tried to tell her about giant squid and the Kraken but she just wanted to go home.
Giant squid can be as long as forty-three feet, which is longer than a bus.
We'd watched 'The Little Mermaid' and mom had got Jenny one of those transfer sets with all the characters so she just stayed inside and did that. The film was alright but transfers are pretty rubbish when there's a beach and jumping insects and animals hiding under stuff.

Mom didn't like the film. She said it was offensive to get obvious actors to speak in stereotype accents instead of just giving the jobs to people who actually come from the places. I think she meant the crab that sounded like uncle Lenny when he's drunk.
Dad said she could take the fun out of anything.

That was last summer and we were in Ireland staying with Mom's aunty Rose. She's me and Jenny's great aunty but I couldn't see why she was so great.

Except she did have dogs. Two massive German Shepard dogs called George and Ringo and I got to take them for walks on the beach and they'd fetch bits of wood from the sea when I threw them. It was brilliant. They'd keep doing it all afternoon til I got tired.

Dogs can't sweat properly. They have to do it through their tongue. That's why you see them panting like crazy when it's hot. They still run around though.

We haven't got a dog. They're not allowed in the block. Cats either. It wouldn't be fair, they'd have to get the lift down just to go and wee. We've got three fish. One each.

Mine's Bruce Wayne.

He's not as big as the other two but he's clever.

There used to be four but dad's fish died 13 days ago, the day after he left.

Top Best things.
1. Writing stories
2. Maradon
3. Batman
4. Going up to the roof
5. Jessica Brown

The roof is mine and Dad's secret. We don't do much else together so whenever we go up there, whether the weather is lovely or ugly the time always feels like treasure.

It's all about stories. We sit on the edge and I tell him what I've been writing or have written and he listens til I'm finished then usually takes a minute before he tells me what he thinks. Sometimes he brings up books that he likes and we take turns reading bits and I get the strange feeling he's different up there.

From so high up we can spy on the passers by and we try and make up stories to go with their lives. Dad is always really good at it and I remember looking at him that time we sat laughing at the man way below us with the funny walk and thinking he looked happy. I didn't say anything though.

Granddad came 10 days ago. He's Mom's dad and used to live here before I was born, then he left to go back to Jamaica.

Jamaica is an island, which is hot and could fit thirteen times into Great Britain. Mom says that even the rain is warm so when you go out in it, it feels like one big shower for everyone. She says the air is different and you feel it run into your lungs as soon as you step off the plane.

I've never been there, but the clock in the kitchen is shaped like Jamaica. It's made of light brown wood the same colour as a caramac bar and is varnished and the hands are really thin and a goldy metal colour. It's hard to tell the time because there are no numbers on it, just names of towns and areas. Granddad is from is where ten o'clock should be, a place called Chester Castle, fourteen miles south west of Montego Bay.

Mom goes out there every summer to see family and help organise things.

It costs a lot of money to get there cos you have to fly and that's why she goes on her own, usually for three weeks, but it always feels like forever.

Granddad's here to help mom and look after Jenny and me because Mom works far away and leaves early in the morning and only gets back in time for dinner.

Yesterday I came home thinking about what had happened in class; Granddad must've seen it in my face. He sat down and asked me to explain. So I did.

About how I was trying to draw the claws of the boss monster from my latest story when I looked up and saw her, sitting two seats in from the corner. How I had to ask somebody her name and how it felt like she just appeared at the exact same time that I saw her and how all I wanted was more of her. How the clock was above her head and it said half past two and the last few claws of my monster never got drawn cos it suddenly felt like the whole class knew that I was staring and Granddad said, fine. Other grown ups would have told me I was being silly, that nothing happens so quickly, but I've seen films, I know what it means. It means she takes over my dreams and that it always seems like she can make things better and Granddad said, fine. When I asked if he thought I was being foolish and whether being in love so quick was stupid he said,

- Son. It doesn't take a whole day to recognize sunshine.

When I asked him why Dad left he said,

- Some people don't know what they have until they lose it.

Granddad talks like that sometimes.

He says things in a way that don't really make sense but let me know that I'm not supposed to ask any more questions.

I remember the night before he left. Mom had stormed off to Aunt Cynthia's and Jenny was asleep. He called me into the living room and we watched Robocop on video even though it's an 18 and we both knew Mom wouldn't like it.
We sat in the dark and watched in silence and I tried not to look away in the bits that got really violent like when the man gets in the acid and he's melting and saying 'Help me!' and the car runs him over.

I knew it was a treat so when it was over and I'd brushed my teeth I went back to say thanks, but dad was fast asleep in his chair. I told myself I wasn't scared and that I was keeping my torch in bed just to be prepared.

<u>Reasons why people leave.</u>
1.There's somewhere better for them to be
2.They did something wrong
3.Somebody did something wrong to them
4.They're scared
5. They bang their head and lose their memory and get amnesia like Michael Knight

The flat smells different now. A mix of Granddad's aftershave, soap and the vegetables that he brings back from his allotment that hang in a red and white striped plastic bag on the hook inside the pantry.

I like Granddad. He talks like uncle Lenny and uncle Roger and his voice is warm and he always wears a vest underneath his shirt and you can see it cos his shirts are thin and never wrinkled like my school shirt and he smells like the aftershave from the dark green bottle with the long neck and last night he let me put some on. The bottle said 'for men' which means I'm a man, even though I'm not eleven til May. He tipped a little bit into my palm and told me to rub my hands together and splash it onto my cheeks and neck, so I did and it felt like somebody set fire to my skin. Granddad wears special shoes that don't make any sound when he walks so he can sneak up on you whenever he wants, like a ninja.

A ninja is an assassin, which means they kill people for money and they wear black so you can only see their eyes and they move in silence and kill you with ninja stars or some of the wire they use to cut cheese.

In the morning he makes breakfast for me and Jenny, dumpling, beans, bacon if there is any or sometimes fish fingers.

This morning he tried to get us to eat this stuff called acky, but it was like snot and me and Jenny couldn't eat it so we just had Frosties.

I've only seen him eat once and he went really slowly, like he was thinking about every fork-full. He chewed like he really meant it and just like his shoes, his mouth didn't make any sound.

I've been leaving before him and Jenny in the morning so I can get to the bus stop in time for 7:40.

After school I play football til half four, then get into town in time for five to catch him leaving through those frosted glass doors.

When I get home I go straight to my room and put my notepad in the shoebox under my bed, then go through to the kitchen, have some Vimto and join in with whatever game Granddad and Jenny are playing. Either; gin rummy with granddad's shiny deck, tic-tac-toe with the pebbles from the kitchen drawer, Connect 4 or Dominoes. Granddad can hold all seven in one hand and he knows which ones you're holding without even looking. I don't know how he does it; I can only hold four and then they slip out. He says practise makes perfect.

I think he lets Jenny win but I don't tell her that.

I haven't told him about my mission. I haven't told Jenny or Mom either. I won't tell anyone til I find out enough then I'll get them all together and explain.

Today will be lunchtime tracking number three and I'll see if he does the same thing. Walk through town ignoring all the shops and he only stops outside the jewellers. Twice now I've seen him go right up to the glass so his nose almost touches the window. He doesn't go in though. After a minute or so he carries on, usually faster, like a dog getting away from his master and I have to speed up but not make it obvious that I'm following. Which is hard, because if he stops I have to carry on so I look natural when in actual fact my reactions have trapped me cos I can't look back and that happening is exactly why I need practise.

He goes to a small shop that looks messy with an old glass and green door and looking through the window I've never ever seen more records or books or films in one place. All the walls, half the floor and even the windowsills are filled with a million covers, some older than others, some different versions of the same thing and as he goes in the bell on the door sounds with the same ring.

I pretend to browse through the glass and as the lunchtime town crowd moves past behind me I try and see what's happening inside. The man who works in the shop always stops what he's doing when he walks in and they start talking and do a funny handshake that looks like it takes practise and must mean they're friends.

The shop man has darker side-parted hair and a rough sort of beard and looks sort of weird like he's always nearly angry, but handsome, like someone from a film.

Then they go to the pub and I can't follow, so I think from tomorrow I'll stop coming at lunchtime.

It was 10 days ago. The day Granddad came, after dinner, Mom sent me to the outdoor for bin bags and peanut brittle and on the way back I took a little detour and went up to the roof for the first time on my own. I did what Dad would never let me and climbed onto the ledge and walked right along the edge looking down and that's when I saw him. Walking towards the main doors, the man I've seen a couple of times before, who lives across the hall and the idea hit me.

I quickly ran down the metal stairs, back into the hall, called the lift, reached our floor and sprinted to our door just as I heard the other lift doors open.

I stood on the yellow pages to see through the peephole. It seemed to take ages before he reached number 15 and put his key in the keyhole. As he stepped inside he looked back and I really thought he could see me and I nearly fell off the phonebook, but the feeling

I got made it easy. This was what I had to do.

Now it's day nine and I reckon in three or four more days time, I'll be ready to start writing.

Plan.
1. Follow man from number 15 and people close to him
2. Become expert private detective by watching films and reading books on subject
3. Write best ever story
4. Find out where Dad went
5. Give Dad story

Now where's this bus?

Part Three

Monday.

We'd gone to the park cos it snowed and Dad showed me how to build a barricade.

A barricade is a wall you build to protect yourself.

He built one too and we had a snowball war. He taught me about strategy and how you have to be ready, but then I got tired and he caught me off guard and threw a hard one just as I looked out and before I heard him shout duck, I'd been knocked down.

That was my first black eye. This is my second.

The others said it was an accident, but I know that he meant it.

He's jealous about Jessica and

There's only me and him could've bent it over there heads round the wall full force and put it exactly where we wanted.

There were four in the wall, all pretty tall, so I didn't know it was coming right for me til it was too late.

Straight in my face and it went numb.

The wall parted and even with one eye I could see in his face he knew exactly what he'd done.

We just stood, like cowboys, waiting for me to cry. The side of my face started tingling like it was made of ice.

I just walked past him and went inside.

In the glass door of the sick room I could see my face was red on one side and I felt my mouth start to smile.

Then, as I sat down I touched my face and felt something wet. The ice had melted.

I had cried, I just hadn't felt it.

In the bus window now I can see my reflection with one dark eye as buildings move past behind it.

Today I wait for him outside his office building and get him to explain what he was doing on the roof yesterday. How does he know? And why did he take her?

It didn't matter that I got into town late on Friday. As I came round the corner before the jewellers, there he was, same as always, staring, and that's when the daring started.

Do it.

Just walk over and speak.

And say what? Hello, you don't know me, but I've been watching you closely for just over a week. I live across the hall and I'm not a stalker I'm writing a story and-

Then he actually went in.

I moved closer and lent on a post box.

He came out holding a small plastic bag and moved off, not as fast as normal, more thoughtful, and his face looked like Jenny's does when she wins at Connect 4.

I followed him round to his friends shop.

Standing across the street by a black van I was imagining Hannibal and BA in the front seat.

You know you want to go in. Go over and open the door. You can find out loads if you can hear what they're saying, are you doing this for real or are you just playing?

I felt a long breath leaving my mouth as I crossed over the road,

then just as I got close enough to open the door I saw the sign change from open to closed as the shop man's hand turned it over. I could see his face, he looked angry and for a second I thought he looked at me so I turned away.

Looking back through the glass bit on the door, I saw them talking. The shop man was shaking his head and walking around while the other man just stood holding the bag from the jewellers.

I moved out of the way as they came out. One man smiling, the other with a frown and as they walked away together the shop man's head turned round and stared, just for a second but, I'm telling you, that time it definitely felt like he was sending a message.

Stay Away

I got back to class late.

I told Miss Burly the Doctors was really busy.

She bought it, and told me to choose a seat then, as she started talking to the class about our animal reports, something caught my eye.

The new kid was sitting over by the window right next to Jessica Brown. Cos of my story I was late and he'd made a move for her. What are you waiting for Mr Gardener, applause? The class laughed and I felt my face go red and all I wanted was to smash his head on the radiator, then he waved at me to come sit with them. He'd saved me a seat.

I'd thought he was being really sneaky but it was just me being mean.

I looked at Jessica quickly, but she was too pretty so I looked down. I could feel the excitement of being near her starting in my feet.

In a way, him being in between us made it easier cos it meant she couldn't really see me.

She had this pen that I've never seen with red, black, blue and green sliding buttons on the top and when you pressed a button you could write in a different colour.

My pencil looked rubbish.

The new kid was making conversation as he drew his Bengal Tiger. He didn't seem bothered that he was sitting right beside her and as she sat talking, while writing about the natural habitat of the golden eagle, I started to find it easier to breathe.

He looked at the title on my report 'The Nomads of the North',
Did you know polar bears cover their own noses when they go hunting? That way they're completely white against the snow so they can get really close before the seals know.

Jessica seemed impressed, so I did my best not to correct him. See I know about polar bears and that fact isn't true it's just something that people made up cos it sounds cool. I could have told them a better one, the fact that Polar Bears are the only animal on the planet with no natural predator except themselves and man and man can't eat polar bear meat because there are things in it called enzymes that can kill us. Basically, like an animal superhero, nobody messes with a polar bear.

She asked him why he'd come half way through the year and he told us what had happened.

She didn't seem shocked and then she told us about how her dad had been killed in a car crash last summer. She had the saddest face I've ever seen as she told us how he'd been walking on Three Shires Oak road and hadn't seen a silver Cortina come between

two parked cars from the side and take him.
That kind of stopped the conversation and in the space, I could've told them about Dad leaving, but I didn't.

We walked home together, the three of us, and for some reason it seemed normal.
We were talking about Danny Jones and how some of the other kids were saying that the new kid had hit him even though we knew different.
As I talked she was really listening and I was watching her lips and thinking they looked like little bits of tangerine and imagining kissing them.
The sky was two different greys as she walked the other way glancing back with a smile.

The new kid's house was the one with the really big wooden front door and it was crazy to actually go in to a place I've walked past on my way home ever since I was four. There was an old rug that covered the hall floor and I could smell furniture polish and perfume. He said his aunty was asleep in the front room so we went upstairs.
There was a Batmobile poster on his door and looking round the room I'd never ever seen more toys or books or films in my life. The toys looked like they'd never been touched and some of the films were 15s and 18s like, Gremlins and Predator and Nightmare on Elm St and it must mean he's allowed to watch them on his own.
It was like somebody had decided he could live like a grown up.

He told me I could take anything I wanted and pointed to one corner where there were a couple of Christmas presents he hadn't even opened and I noticed a framed photo of the Joker next to his bed.

He went over and lay down, as I moved round from one thing to another like a playground. He seemed bored as I sat on the floor and opened a Shoot magazine from a pile that had never been read, he just lay staring at the ceiling then said,
"I'm gonna think about her when I wank later".

Things I know about the New Kid.
1.　He knows how to play football properly
2.　He's not scared of girls
3.　He drinks his calypso by biting a hole in the bottom and squeezing it instead of using the straw
4.　He lives in the posh house
5.　He watched a mugger kill his mom and dad last Christmas

Today is the same as always. The bus is nearly empty. Just the old man and woman who sit down near the front and say nothing the whole way, and me.
Why were they sitting on the edge of the roof?

I was on my own in the flat on Sat morning. Granddad had gone to the allotment before I got up and Mom and Jenny had gone into town to buy Jenny new shoes. The ones from the girly advert with the fairies. They've got a little key that's supposed to be for the door

to a secret garden stuck in the heel. Everybody knows it's not real, I mean even if you found the door, how could you open it with the key glued inside your shoe? I didn't tell Jenny that.
I was sat on the sofa watching Gordon the Gofer annoying Philip Schofield on the telly.
Dad's chair was empty.
Nobody really sits there now but I could hear him trying to tempt me.
I sat down and sank into the cushion and straight away it felt like I shouldn't have done it.
I felt small, like when I used to sit in his footprints in the snow.
But different.
Philip Schofield told the boy who'd phoned in he hadn't won.
I shuffled to get out then felt something uncomfortable pushing the side of my bum.
I felt under the cushion and pulled it out.
It wasn't mine, but I recognized it.
Black with an elastic band holding it closed. I know you're not supposed to go through someone else's notes but he told me to do it. Just read the first page you don't have to go through it.
I sat up straight and pulled the elastic band off gently
Every page was the same.
Empty.
There was no one to tell me I wasn't supposed to so I ate peanut butter and square crisps for breakfast and thought about my day, follow the lady from number 15 then come home and piece together the things that I've seen.

She sat down near the front, where the old couple are now. Brown handbag, a long black coat and that scarf over a dark blue dress.
I decided to risk it and sat right behind her.
She smelt like my bed and it felt nice just being near her. Her head leaning against the window, her hair was the colour of wood and I wanted to touch it.
Then we reached town.
I knew where she was going I just didn't know why. That same shop with all the records, books and films inside. It was closed.
She went right up til her nose touched the glass and I wanted to ask her why she was looking for the shop man. I passed her and stood leaning on a lamppost and if she'd looked over her shoulder she would've seen me.
I could see the air she was breathing steaming up the window.
That's condensation.
Condensation is what happens when something warm touches something cold.
You get water.
She just stood looking and I could feel her brain working. Part of her hair was across her face like Roger Rabbit's girlfriend.

Then she moved on, this time faster. Like a dog getting away from its master, but I'm really good at this now so I knew that as long as I could still see her, letting her get further away wasn't a disaster.
So at first I kept my distance, outside Smiths whistling. She went left, checked back, went right and crossed over. And I got closer. So close I could almost touch her shoulder.

Then she went into a pub.

Looking through the window I saw her go into the toilet. Inside was smoky and full of old men playing dominoes.

There was a little telly up on a shelf showing horse racing and two men were making faces and waving their fists. Then I noticed the ones sitting down were all holding all their dominoes in one hand.

She came out, counted some change in her hand, walked to the pay phone then changed her mind.

I followed her all the way up the high street, past McDonalds, past the road his office is on, out of town to the park.

She went into the phone box by the little kids playground.

I wanted to know more so I moved round to the opposite side to the door where she couldn't see me, but I could just about make out her voice say, 'I need to see you'. Then she hung up. I waited til she came out then, when she moved away, I made sure I went the other way round.

She sat on the bench just past the swings. There was a man pushing two little girls one with each hand. They were laughing and had matching coats.

I was fed up of hiding and walked over and sat down on the other end of the bench.

She took something out of her handbag. It looked like a pen but she didn't hold it like one. She stared at it then put it back.

The fingers on her left hand moved strands of dark hair behind her right ear.

I felt weird.

- Don't I know you?

She said looking over. And I didn't even feel like I'd blown it.

- Maybe. My name's David.

She smiled and I forgot to breathe.

- Yeah. I know you. I sometimes see you in the mornings. You go to our juniors don't you? I've read your work on the wall. You're the boy who writes the stories.

Then there she was. Jessica, sitting on her own on one of the swings. The strange thing was I hadn't noticed her approaching. She hadn't noticed me either. Her thin metal headphones blocking out the sound.

She smiled and moved them round her neck as I sat down on the swing next to hers. I smiled back and we just sat with no messy words.

It felt different to school. Just the two of us, out of uniform, on a Saturday afternoon.

- I watch you sometimes.

She leant her head against the grey metal chain. She had light blue jeans and her grey jumper was a little bit too big but perfect.

- I know.

I asked her what she was listening to and she told me to get closer so I could hear.

It was a tape her dad made her of a man called Neil. We sat with our swings leaning and heads together and nothing moved.

'I have a friend I've never seen. He hides his head inside a dream'

When I got back to our block it was gone seven o'clock but I was too excited to have an excuse, and that's when I saw him, waiting, Looking up at the flats.

He looked different at night. His hair wasn't side parted anymore and he looked like he was getting ready for something as he sat on the wall staring up.

I went to move behind the main doors but he came towards me with that same stare from outside his shop.

I held my breath and pretended to look for my keys. As he came closer I smelled the pub and I wanted to hide, but it was no good.

But he wasn't bothered about me. He went over to the lift pushed the button and stood watching his feet.

I told myself that this was one of those moments when you can either show what you're made of or prove that you're hopeless.

Like Dad said about Maradona,

- Great players make things happen.

I walked over as the lift doors opened, showing no panic.

He stared at the buttons then pressed the one for our floor and as the doors closed the lift smelled like the pub.

When it moves it usually makes my stomach move with it, but this time I couldn't tell if it was the lift or who was stood in it.

Then, it was like the little numbers that light up above the doors were the source of my power as we went up the floors, and I wasn't scared.

The doors opened and I stepped out, but he just stood there frozen. His eyes looked down and his mouth opened, but before he could say anything the doors closed.

It's just before 5.

I'm bang on time.

It's colder than it looked through the window. I wish I had my coat and that sounds like a siren.

There's a crowd of people in the road outside his building.

They're all stood around something. I get nearer.

> I wanna see, but I can't get through, there are no spaces to squeeze in between, the people are packed too close. They look serious.
>
> I look up and think of the The Joker falling.
>
> The sky is one kind of grey and someone says, it's too late, he's not going to make it.

<u>Things a great story needs.</u>
1. A baddy
2. A girl
3. Someone trying to do something
4. Something you don\t understand that becomes clear later
5. Someone to die

Part Four

Everything was touched with orange from the lamppost outside. The swirls of paint on the artex ceiling looked like deep whipped cream and as she lay fast asleep next to me I wanted to reach up and feel it.

I heard her mumble something and felt her body moving rolling over throwing her left arm over her shoulder and whack! She hit me. She didn't even wake up as I sat up holding my face and I watched as she curled into a ball somehow taking up most of the space on the mattress.

This morning went quickly.

I came in, people stared shared a joke asking who'd hit me. I told Mavis I'd opened a door into my own face and she bought it, told me my education had been wasted. Jane offered to make me a tea but sat down again when Mavis told her stupidity didn't deserve sympathy. Malcolm just looked over the top of his monitor and smiled like he knew what I was going to do.

Dean went into his usual routine, this time he was particularly pleased because he'd got some girl into bed and only spent a fiver. He didn't care if I was listening as he walked away punctuating his latest tale with a cocky smile and,
- Nice Shiner

I didn't mind.

This time tomorrow I won't be here.

We were in the smoking room making tea when I told the boss I was leaving.
She was taking the piss about my eye asking if I wanted her to kiss it better.
I just did what I always do and let her carry on thinking about how, if roles were reversed and I was her boss, I'd probably have lost my job.
She didn't believe me. She waited for me to say it was a joke and when I didn't her smile broke and she told me that I was supposed to give two weeks notice and if I left today I'd owe two weeks pay.
- Ok.
I said.
And she walked away.
The metal handle of the teapot burned my fingers as I poured.
I told myself if I let go before my mug was full Jess would die.

He never phones, especially not at work. He sounded like he'd been drinking when he told me he'd walk over and meet me outside at five.

The numbers above the doors say the lift is down in reception and I've already pressed the button so all I can do is wait. Something I've been doing every day since I came here. I won't have to look at that clock anymore. That clock, that can make two minutes take an hour if you look at it in the wrong way.

My days are gonna be different now. I know I've got enough saved to not have to work for about six months and that's gonna have to be enough to get most of the writing done.

I knew what he'd say when I showed him the ring. I was ready for it so I just stood steady and let him rant. I knew he wouldn't give me a chance to speak so I just waited. He locked the shop door and laid it out. How all I was doing was ruining my way out, how I'd been like this since the playground, how all it would mean would be the end of excitement, safe David strikes again making bold gestures cos he's frightened.
I didn't mind. Everything feels different and I know he can tell. So after about five minutes of pacing and his face changing colour, he stopped.
- Riley, I love her.
He shrugged and I asked him to come out with us for Chinese later and he tried to do his usual, *I can't make it*
but I made him agree.

The three of us sat in a dark red booth eating hot and sour soup and noodles. One beauty in the middle of two stooges as we talked about how we used to do stuff together all the time.
I had Saturday planned and my hands wouldn't stay still as I fumbled with my chopsticks moving my noodles.
Riley said *things change. You used to write stories.*
Jess looked at him then at me and said nothing.
- I'm thinking of writing a new one.
Both their faces changed and he coughed as a little bit of soup went down the wrong way.
What did you say?

- I said I'm gonna write a story. I had an idea.
Jess smiled. Then the fortune cookies arrived.

I remember the three of us walking back from nights out in a University town. Clothes stuck to our backs from four hours dancing to Northern Soul and only noticing the sweat as we stepped out into the cold.
Nineteen years old.
Not really knowing what we were doing but enjoying not being told.
I remember how he'd look at her as she pulled on her coat.
Like he used to at school.
Like he still does now.

I went through my desk this morning. Four years and they only thing I found that I wanted to take with me was a worn piece of A4 with two eleven man, all time fantasy football teams that me and Malcolm did nearly three years ago.
Most of his players were older than mine but we both only chose players who could change a game. A lot of people say you need muscle in midfield. The yin to balance the yang of you skill player, but the best players do it all; win the ball, play it simple and short or maraud forward and terrorise the back four. They can be both.
Great players make things happen.
It would've been a great game; battles all over the pitch and both number tens with exactly the same name.
Diego Armando Maradona.

I lay pretending to be half asleep when Jess left for town on Saturday morning.

I waited for enough time for the lift to reach down and her to be out, then I was up.

All the stuff from the living room went into the bedroom, except the sofa, which got pushed against one wall. When I'd put the 20-kilogram bag of sand round the side of the block on Friday nobody saw. Getting it up in the lift would've been hard if I hadn't been so excited. I tipped it out onto the cheap laminated floor and, with my hands, spread it out so it covered all but a strip along the opposite wall to the sofa.

The dark blue sheets we never use lay in that strip and became the ocean.

With the windows open the breeze blew the leaves of the yucca plant we bought the day we moved which was now a palm tree swaying calmly in the tropical air.

The wall was the best bit. I've got a scanner and work had a projector and nobody had batted an eyelid when I walked out Friday with it under my arm and when I got home I would've told Jess I had a presentation to prepare, but she didn't even notice. The photo we took of the sun setting into the sea in Cornwall finished the scene.

Our living room was a beach.

In the kitchen I made up a jug of my version of strawberry Daiquiri and didn't hold back on the rum, changed into my t-shirt and shorts, hit the repeat button on the 'Sounds of the Sea' CD I'd bought and sat on the sofa, my toes in the cold sand, one hand holding half a coconut of badly mixed liquor, the other gripping a little velvet box in my hip pocket and waited for Jess to come home.

By the time I heard her key in the door it really was sunset and I was on my fourth daiquiri. She dropped her handbag and stood in the doorway.
I'm not sure what happened first, whether I tried to get up or she starting crying.
The door opening had made a space in the sand like a slice of pie and that's where she stood as I took out the box and opened it looking up into her eyes.

The pair of us sat, side-by-side on a towel on the sand on our living room floor looking at the view we'd seen when we were seventeen. The breeze from the open window was turning cold as I told her about my idea.
She liked it, but even more she liked that I'm thinking about writing. We sat with our backs against the sofa, looking over at our frozen moment sipping our bad daiquiris and she wrapped herself around me.

When I woke up she wasn't there.
The bedroom window was wide open and it was cold and I could hear birds and as I sat holding my pounding head I felt bits of sand in my hair.
Cornwall flickered as I switched the projector off.
Then I heard the kettle.
She came in with tea and toast, and we sat on the sofa.

She was holding her mug with both hands and I noticed the ring.
- It fits.
- Of course it does
And she sipped her tea, knees up next to her chest wearing her knickers and vest and I got a flashback of her dropping her daiquiri as she got on top of me, then it was gone.
- I'll clean this up later. When my headache goes.
- Leave it.
She said
- I like it in between my toes.

I hadn't been up to the roof since we moved out of the block into our first house that summer before secondary school. I remember trying to get used to not sleeping on the same floor as the main door and Jenny and Granddad playing drawn on connect four on the grey walls before we all painted over them.

We weren't even fully dressed when we got into the lift, but Jess didn't question it.
We left the metal door open and stepped out onto the flat concrete. The light hurt our eyes with no buildings to hide behind and it hit me just how close to the sky it feels up there.
We sat on the edge and I told her what I remembered.
- I remember it being important. I remember sitting right here on the edge looking down and making up stories and I remember feeling warm.

The wind was blowing her hair as she sat staring at me. I'd seen that look before,
- I want to tell you why I was so late yesterday
But before she could say any more
somebody slammed the roof door.

One time I thought I saw my dad. In town coming out of the station. I think it was him. It was just before Christmas a couple of years ago. Course there's no way to know now cos I didn't go over, I just froze. He looked smaller. The skin on his face looked loose and what was left of his hair was grey. He didn't see me and I remember feeling glad. He could've lived a million miles away or on the other side of town for all it mattered.

Last night I lay in the bath. Planning.
First thing I'm gonna do is buy a notebook. A proper one.
Black moleskin.
The lift doors open and I step inside. There's no need for goodbyes. There lives won't change in the absence of mine and to be honest I haven't got time.

When I came out of the bath in my towel she was lying on the sofa and I looked at the TV and recognised the start of the film. She knows it's my favourite.
- I saved you a space.

As the doors go to close something stops them.
It's Malcolm.

He shakes my hand handing me something, smiles, says
- Thank you
Then turns and walks away.
As the lift doors close I look down at my hand and see a pen.

By the time it reached the final scene Jess was asleep.
Batman and the Joker on top of the cathedral and I knew every word.
- 'I'm going to kill you.'
- 'You idiot. You made me remember?'….
I remember Riley.
I made you. But I don't need you anymore.
Walking across reception for the last time I've never felt this sure
I hear the sirens.
People are standing in the road
They're all crowded around something.
I move past and
I could look over their tightly packed shoulders
But I don't need to.

There is a boy. His name is David.
David writes stories.
This is his.

Return
(2009)

produced by BAC
script development and dramaturgy by Yael Shavit
design by Marie Blunck
live sound score and arrangement by
Daniel Marcus Clark

- This is wrong

- What do you mean?

- I mean it's not fair Saul, look at him

- He loves it. Don't you Dom?

- Mom's gonna go mad. That's her best lipstick

- Stop whining, Noreen

- Don't call me that! She'll know it was your idea

- Good. Pass me that powder stuff

- Am I a lady yet?

- Not yet big man. Nearly though, you look lovely.

- No, He looks like a midget drag queen

- Don't listen to him, Dom

- What's a drag queen?

- Well done, Noah

- I'm phoning social services

- Just shut up and tell me what you think will ya?

(beat)

- His hair's wrong

- Wrong?

- It's not girly enough, you've gotta poof it up more.

- What?

- Gimme the comb. I'll do it. Right, sit still Dom

THURSDAY.

EXT. NEW STREET STATION. NIGHT.

A young man sits in the drivers seat of a dark blue, 1995 Volkswagen golf. He is in his late teens. He smokes a cigarette, muttering to himself. The edge of his dark wiry hair pokes out from under his light grey hood. His fingers drum the steering wheel.

Through the windscreen we see a stream of people begins to emerge through the station's glass doors. The young man winds down the window, flicks the cigarette and sits forward.

Amongst the crowd of people we see a man in his late twenties wearing his grey hoody pulled up under his brown jacket. He carries an old hold all. The young man honks the horn. As he starts the engine the passenger side door opens and the older man gets in.

- Noah
- Dominic. So this is it?
- Yeah
- Nice ride
- Ride? Where are you from?
- Sorry, nice Whip
- We're not Amercian, Noah
- I'm joking, Dom
- I know

- Look at you, all big and driving. Is that a moustache?

The pair of them stare out through the windscreen. The car waits in a queue.

- You look tired Noah
- That's what hard work does to you.
- Yeah right.

Dominic takes out a packet of cigarettes.

- What? You smoke now? Does mom know?
- Jesus, Noah. Welcome back.

The car pulls out onto the city streets. An array of fast-food colours and tall buildings. Young men and women walk in packs with interlinking arms laughing and shouting.

- You out tonight then?
- What? With this lot? You kidding? I'm from here remember? Not really my thing Noah. Besides I'm picking you up aren't I?

Dominic flicks his ash out of the slit of open window

- Mom's made dinner. Yours is in the oven. Probably rock solid by now.
- I'm not coming home.

- What?

- I'm gonna stop at Granddad's

- Oh. Mom's not gonna like that. She's been on about it all week. You should see your room.

- She'll be fine. I'll be over tomorrow. Just take me to Granddad's alright?

The car moves through an underpass. Artificial light turns everything pale. Noah stares out of the window his head against the glass. They drive past the woods. Streetlights catch the edges of old trees and beyond them darkness stretches out.

- You going up past the George?

- No, they made it one way, I gotta go up Thimblemill

- Thimblemill?

Dominic smiles

- You're out of touch

- I'm fine. Do a right at the island

- Yes, Noah. I do know where I'm going

We zoom out through the windscreen, up above the moving car as it approaches an island. Its headlight antennae feel the dark night in front as it circles round and moves off along a quiet street.

INT. 9TH FLOOR OF A TOWER BLOCK. NIGHT.

A young woman turns her key in the flat door in slow motion. She slides the key out and steps inside. Hanging her coat on the hook she walks through to a living room lit by a large flat screen television. The rest of the room is modest. In the blue light from the screen we see the woman is in her early/mid twenties. She is attractive in a manga comic book kind of way. Her dark hair pulled back in a ponytail. On the worn sofa sits a teenage girl.

- Hey
- Hey. Have you even moved?
- Course I have. Tea don't make itself, Eve. You look tired
- I am tired Sam, some of us have to work. What you watching?

Eve slides off her shoes.

- It's Wife Swap, come and sit down. Look, check out this idiot. He's having a go at her cos she won't clean up after him like his real wife does. I tell ya Eve, you'd piss in his tea

EXT. QUIET TERRACED STREET. NIGHT.

The Volkswagen pulls away and the street is still. Light from the lamppost makes the pristine flowers glow radioactive.

Noah walks up the narrow garden path to the side of the house. He ignores the council front door and heads to the black wooden back gate.

At the back of the house he runs his hand along the top framing of the door and a key drops to the floor by his feet. He looks out at the garden. The small kept lawn looks like carpet in the dark. framed with a skirting of perfectly balanced plants. Noah smiles and starts to peel off his shoes.

Inside he sits on the old brown sofa.

The carriage clock's second hand beats a slow metronome between old photos and cheap porcelain animals. Light from outside leaks through net curtains touching the edges of dated furniture. To the left on the wall behind the tv we see an a framed picture of two boys in their pants standing in a back garden, both soaking wet, their arms around each other's shoulders. One of them is slightly older with cropped hair. He wears an ear-to-ear grin with one front tooth missing as he stares out. The younger boy is smiling too, but his smile is closed and his dark hair longer. He looks up at the older boy. We hear voices.

- You're doing it wrong.
- What do you mean?
- You're doing it wrong. Look it's crumbling as you cut it.
- It's hard.
- You've gotta do it right. You're not doing it right.

- How do I do it?
- Give me the knife. Look. You find your slice, alright? You choose the width. Doorstop, best sandwiches are doorstop. Nice and thick, yeah?
- Yeah.
- Right, so you've got your line. Now you start.
- That's what I did.
- No. I haven't told you the trick yet.
- What trick?
- There's a way to do it right. Dad showed me.
- Dad?
- You can't stop.
- What?
- You can't stop. Once you start you can't stop. Not for a second. You choose your line, you start and you keep going.
- It's working.
- I know. That's what you have to do. Look, the perfect slice. Now you try.
- I'll mess it up.
- I'll mess it up, just choose your line.
- I feel like I'm in school.
- You are in school, Noah. Now learn. That's it, you're doing it.
- It's hard.
- Course it's hard. Just keep going.
- I'm doing it, Saul.
- I know you are. Now hurry up I'm hungry.

Noah extends his leg bringing his right foot into view. His bare toes carry a few stray blades of grass. As we focus in, between his toes he sees the older boy with the missing tooth smile staring out. Noah looks up towards the room above him, hearing muffled snores through the floorboards perfectly in synch with every other tock.

INT. KITCHEN. LATE

A fridge door opens and from inside we see Dominic's face glow in the light of the tiny bulb. His young moustache looks darker in the half-light. The shelves inside are bleached white and hold nothing but an opened pack of anchor butter, half a bottle of milk, eggs and a packet of bacon. As Dominic takes out the milk and shuts the door we hear the kettle begin to boil. Through the open back door the night is dark.
On the sideboard a torn half of an a4 piece of lined paper says, *Welcome home Noah. There's stew in the oven, mom x* Dominic crushes the note in his hand and drops it into the metal bin. From outside the window we see him move to the kettle, spoon four sugars into an empty mug and take out a cigarette.   Fade to black.

VOICE OVER:

You fight to get out. Convincing yourself as you go that a place is holding you back. That something is waiting for you outside. They don't understand you here and no matter what they think you are, you always have this little splinter inside your head reminding you that things aren't what they could be. So you leave. You break things. You cut ties and go.

What you don't realise is that there is nothing waiting for you, but you. An older you, mouthing words, staring out of windows, losing sleep, forgetting to dream. Nothing stops. What you leave carries on. The space where you were gets filled with something else and night becomes day. Just like it always has.

'RETURN'

FRIDAY.
INT. LIVING ROOM. EARLY MORNING.

We hear the crackle of bacon in a pan before the fade up to horizontal extreme close up of the side of Noah's face.
His left eye twitches under it's lid, the beginnings of lines in his forehead and we see an old crescent-shaped scar millimeters from the corner of the eye, one shade lighter than the skin in sits in.
A kettle begins to whistle and the eye slowly opens.

INT. KITCHEN. EARLY MORNING.

An old man stands at the stove turning over sausage and bacon in a pan already crammed with eggs and mushrooms with the fingertips of one hand. His face holds handsome features sandblasted. He has paul newman eyes. The darkness from outside seeps in through the window dulling the glow of the weak bulb above his head which can't reach the corners of the room. The crackle of the meat and the whistling kettle's steam cloud his ears as he hums an old tune.

- You'll burn your hands old man.

The old man is startled but hardly shows it. He turns his head only slightly to Noah in the kitchen doorway.

- One day you'll do that and somebody'll die. Then you'll be sorry.

Noah smiles

- But not you eh, Granddad?

He moves to the small table, veneered to look real, and pulls out one of the two poorly made chairs, glancing at the cheap analogue clock. It is 5:30am.

- How long you been up?

The old man lays a plate full of over-cooked food in front of Noah with one hand. He rests the other hand on Noah's shoulder.

- A little while. Welcome home, lad.

INT. CAR. MID MORNING.

A small boy kneels in the back seat of a family saloon car staring out of the window. He's about five. He has jet-black hair. As the car reaches traffic lights a bus pulls alongside into its stop. Through the last window the boy sees Noah. Head against the glass, staring out. Their eyes meet and the boy ducks down out of view.
From inside the car we watch as he slowly lifts his head back up to the window. We see Noah staring. As the light's change to green Noah pulls a monster face. The young boy laughs as the car moves away, leaving the bus behind.

INT. SUPERMARKET. LATE MORNING.

Eve sits at the checkout. Pensioners queue quietly to tinny jingle music. She smiles and makes small talk with an old man as he delicately loads cans of corned beef and spam onto the conveyer belt with old hands. He tells her that her earrings look like the circles you make with sparklers on bonfire night and laughs to himself as she asks if he needs any help with his packing.

- I'll be fine. It's not got to that time just yet.

Eve looks at her watch. The old man shrugs

- Long day?
- Yeah. I'm on til ten. Eleven and a half hours to go.
- Oh Dear. You'll need some cheering up
- Yeah. You gonna tell me a joke? Made it a good one

The old man shakes his head and smiles.

- Oh I'm sorry, bab, I forgot all my jokes a long time ago

EXT. SLEEPY SEMI-DETACHED ROAD. LATE MORNING.

We see Noah cross the road after letting the bus pull away. He looks up and down the row of 1960's semi-detached houses. He double takes on a large double glazed porch half way down then starts walking. The morning sunlight heats his back, but the air is still fresh. As he moves past a house with pebble dashed walls we see an old woman staring out between net curtains. She quickly closes them as Noah stares back at her. Noah smiles.

- Yeah. Fuck you, Mrs. Price.

Two doors down he cuts across the small lawn, treading the overgrown grass and rolls a large plant pot beside the front door revealing an old dirty key.

INT. LIVING ROOM. LATE MORNING.

Dominic lays out on the faded floral sofa wearing grey jogging bottoms and an old white vest flicking channels. We move round slowly. The room looks dated. Textured wallpaper is worn in places and the paper lampshade needs replacing. On the walls there are photographs of boys. We recognise Dominic in a few. We hold on two framed pictures in pride of place above the mantelpiece. One of them shows a younger Noah, wearing graduation robes, holding a rolled up certificate. The other shows three boys. Two in their early teens wearing football team strips holding a trophy with one hand each, while between their legs the third boy, no more than 7 years old pokes his head out smiling. The curtains are closed. We hear the front door. Noah walks in.
He takes in the room, moving around the walls, scanning furniture.

- Fucking hell.
- Morning potty mouth.
- It looks the same.

- Course it does. What did you expect?
- I dunno. Hold on, what are you doing here?
- I live here, Noah.
- Don't be funny. Why aren't you in college?
- Jesus. Welcome back. Come in sit down, put the kettle on.
- Answer me.
- It's Friday. I only have one lecture Friday. At two o'clock. Fucks sake.
- Watch your mouth.
- Piss off Noah. You walk through the door and start barking orders?

Noah moves to the window.

- Where's Mom?

- She went shopping for dinner stuff.

Noah pulls open the curtains. The sunlight washes the TV screen in white. Dominic squints.

- Shit Noah! They're closed for a reason.

Noah turns around.

- But Dominic, what will the neighbours think?

They both smile.

- Who's making a brew?
- You are
- No, you are
- Ok, scissors, paper, stone. Best of three yeah?

INT. KITCHEN. LATE MORNING.

Noah stands at the sink staring out of the window into the messy back garden. We see an old dirty white football nestled in the long grass. Dominic leans out of the open back door. The kettle begins to boil.

- How long you think you'll stay?
- I dunno. Where are the mugs?
- We don't keep em in there now, they're in the corner one. Tea bags are in the one on the right.
- What?
- Next one over. No, to the right. Sugar's in that bowl.
(beat)
- We saw you on the radio that time.
- You saw me?
- I mean we heard you. Do you still do that?
- Sometimes. Not really. It changes. How many sugars?
- So they pay you to talk?
- No. Well, yeah. There's more to it than that.

- Like what?

- Doesn't matter. How many sugars you want?

- Four please

- Four sugars? Jesus Dom

Noah drops tea bags into the mugs and spoons four sugars into both. We hear a bird calling from outside. Dominic takes out a pack of cigarettes.

- Do you think he'll win his appeal this time?
- I dunno. Depends how he's been.
- Does he know your back? Are you gonna go see him?
- I dunno Dom. Lets have one of them
- You don't smoke Noah.

He holds out a cigarette.

-Yeah

Noah brings the cigarette to his mouth

- Neither do you. You got a light?

INT. BEDROOM. LATE MORNING.

Noah stands in the open bedroom doorway. The old hold all hangs from his right hand. Late morning light bleeds through cheap football team curtains. The walls hold large movie posters spaced out neatly and football team photos from shoot magazine. Two single beds sit ten feet apart against either wall. Both perfectly made.

Noah moves his feet across the empty landscape of worn beige carpet to the skinny bookcase. Each shelf is packed with VHS cassette tapes. He slowly runs his index finger along the dusty titled spines pausing at Nico (Above the Law). The other tapes exhale into the extra space as his fingers ease the tape from its place.

We hear a lorry drive past outside. Noah moves back across and sits on the edge of the bed on the right. He drops the hold all at his feet and sighs. His eyes catch part of his reflection in the long mirror on the cheap wardrobe door.

We rotate round to a view of the same bed from above, late afternoon.

A younger Noah lies on his back with one arm behind his head. His hair is longer, his face clean-shaven. His left eye is bruised. Coarse stitches jut out from the thin yellowed skin. A girl lays poured over him, the soft hair of her crown under his chin as they lie in silence. Close up of his hand on the small of her back. His fingers gently twist a loose thread into a ball then release it.

- We could go together, Eve

The girl's eyes close.

Noah stares at the empty bed opposite. The checkered sheet is pristinely folded over. The pillow starched rigid. The wall around the headboard is plastered with flyers for late 80's raves. Quest. Helter Skelter. Sunday Roast. On the wall above the flyers there is a space. A poster is missing. Noah looks down at the old video in his hands

- But why is he better?
- It's not about better Noah. It's more real.
- I dunno, Arnie is pretty big
- Look. Seagal would make Arnie break his own nose with his own fist then twist him round and throw him into Stallone's face.
- What about Van Damme? He's proper.
- You're missing the point Noah. They're not real. It's not about saving the world. It's simple. You mess with Seagal's family and he'll snap your elbow

Noah rolls onto his side and stares across at the empty space.

Underneath the empty bed, light reflects in the matt metal of old dumbbells. On the edge of its varnished headboard rough letters are carved vertically. The scarred wood dulled by time. We read a name. SAUL.

INT. LIVING ROOM. EARLY EVENING.

A circular dining table. Empty plates waiting while Mary says grace. Noah and Dominic sit opposite each other. Dominic pulls a face. Noah glares back at him. Mary opens her eyes on her second amen and watches her sons shovel food mountains in front of them. She smiles, as they eat like dogs.

- Did you see your room?
- I did Mom thanks
- I didn't touch a thing.
- I saw, Mom. Will you pass the beans please, Dom?
- Just like it was
- It's great

Noah spoons green beans onto his plate

- You look tired, Noah
- I feel fine, Mom.
- He's just getting old Mom
- We're all getting old Dominic. Your brother looks tired
- Mom, I'm fine.
- Your eye's healed
- What?
- Your eye. I can hardly see it

Mary looks at Dominic

- Can you see it?

Noah touches the small scar next to his left eye

- It has been a while Mom
- No new scars then?
- No, Mom. These potatoes are lovely, aren't they Dom?
- Yeah. Lovely, Mom
- A mother worries about her sons, Noah
- Mom, I'm fine.
- Are you eating? You know you can't cook
- Mom. I can look after myself
- And work? How's work?
- They pay him to talk, Mom
- Works fine, Mom. Everything's fine
- You look tired
- You said that

Mary moves food with her fork

- I saw that girl. You know, the one always hanging around you
- Don't, Mom
- From the estate. Still works in the supermarket
- Mom, you know her name
- She had you two married off in her head. Silly girl. No, you were always too good for her. I always thought she was more

your brother's type
- Mom, can we change the subject? How's college, Dom?
- What was her name again?
- Mom
- Emma?
- Mom
- Alison?
- Fucks sake! Eve. Her name is Eve.

Dominic looks down. Noah closes his eyes.

- I'm sorry mom. You're right I'm tired. I'm just tired. Oh, Mom, sit down. Please

Mary walks away from the table with her plate. The door to the kitchen closes. Noah sighs. Dominic moves food with his fork.

- Well that didn't take long.
- Shut up, Dom
- No seriously, I mean, she didn't even finish her meal. You've not lost it have you, Noah?
- Shut up, Dominic
- Happy Families
- You want a dig?
- Noah, you hit me in your sleep you better wake up and say sorry

- What?
- You heard me.

Noah smiles.

- Dickhead. That's not the line.
- What you mean?
- Mr. White. Reservoir Dogs yeah? That's not what he says. Have you even seen the film?
- Whatever. You better go speak to her.

Noah stands up slowly

INT. KITCHEN. EVENING.

Noah stands at the sink scrubbing a large pan. Dominic stands to his right drying a colander. The tension is obvious.

- So when were you gonna say?
- Gonna say what?
- That you dropped out of college
- What?
- You heard me.
- I didn't drop out
- No? So why'd Mom just say that you have? Why didn't you tell me?
- I left. I chose to leave, Noah. Waste of time

- Ok. So you've got no time to waste?
- No, I don't. Is that clean yet?
- No, it's not. So what's your plan? I mean seen as how time is so short?
- I got a few things sorted.
- Oh you have. That's good.
- Fuck you, Noah. You don't know anything. You haven't been here. - - - Now you're gonna act all worried
- Who's worried? Do I look worried?
- Is that why you're back?

Noah scrubs the pan. Dominic twists the tea towel round his fist.

- It's all bollocks you know. She just wanted you to come home. Jesus Noah, you'll wear through the metal

Noah stops scrubbing.

- She's worried, Dom. She says you hardly leave the house.
- What? She's worried Noah, but not about me. Jesus, I can't believe that's why you're here.
- I'm here cos I want to be.
- So what? Gimme a lecture on 'seeing things through' then piss off again?
- Stop it, Dom.
- What a joke! Like you could ever lecture me.

- I know what it's like
- You don't know fuck all, Noah! I'm not you. This is so lame.
- I just wanna help
- Fock off! You left! You don't live here. You don't know anything. Now you think you can just breeze in and play the hero? Well it don't suit you, Noah. It never did. You're not Saul.

Noah looks down. The pair of them wash and dry in silence. The hum of the fridge fills the kitchen.
Noah hands Dominic the pan.

- You used to wear that on your head. You remember?
- What?
- You used to wear that pan on your head and get us to call you the 'Knight of the Round Table'. Wooden spoon sword, broom horse. You telling me you don't remember?
- No.
- Ask, Mom. You used to run around telling us all how you were gonna save the day. "Don't worry everybody. I'm here to beat the dragon"

Dominic's face straightens as he moves the towel over the pan.

- That wasn't me, Noah. I've heard Mom tell that story before. That was you.

He drops the tea towel on the draining board and walks out of the kitchen.

INT. SUPERMARKET. NIGHT.

Eve walks along the cereal aisle. As she pushes through the rubber perspex doors she glances up at the company clock. The red digital numbers say 9:20pm. She turns up her collar at the harsh cold of the freezer.

EXT. REAR OF SUPERMARKET. NIGHT.

Industrial lighting throws a blanket on the cracked concrete. We see the fire escape door jerk open. Eve leans with her shoulder on the frame and lights a cigarette. Taking a long drag she exhales watching the smoke float into the night. She looks down at the small lighter in her left hand. It is light blue with fake handwriting and a picture of a fairground on it.
She smiles to herself and, after another drag, she cranes her neck up and tries to blow a ring with the smoke, only producing a small cloud that breaks out into nothing in front of her face.

- You never could do that.

She drops her cigarette. Her face in the foreground, we see

over her shoulder Noah stands in the shadows between palettes stacked with milk. Eve does not turn around. We see her face fight for composure as her foot twists out the half finished Benson. She turns to face him.

- Yeah. Well I had a shit teacher.

INT. SUPERMARKET WAREHOUSE. NIGHT

Eve pulls the fire escape door closed.
The hum of the generator fills the space between them. She eases her hands into her pockets. The high warehouse ceiling lights cast her shadow out in front of her almost reaching him.

- What are you doing here?

Noah takes a step forward.

- I came to see you.

Eve steps back. Her top teeth comb her bottom lip. Her eyes take him in.

- No you didn't.

She walks past him and out into the shop light.

INT. CLUB TOILET. YEARS AGO.

Drops of blood collect into a dark pool around a plughole. We hear the thump of a house bass line through the walls. A younger Noah stares into the dirty toilet mirror holding the side of his face. Blood leaks through his fingers dripping down his arm into the cracked sink. A dark patch covers the chest of his white shirt. Younger Noah moves his hand. We see a deep gash millimetres from the corner of his left eye, the white of bone visible. He reaches for the paper towel dispenser finding only the plastic edge of the empty box.
Loud music bursts in as the door swings open. Noah looks down.
A young skinny man wearing a black shirt and trousers stands in the doorway looking towards Noah

- Yo! We gotta go

Noah leans forward, his nose almost touching the dirty mirror. We see the skin around the cut is retracted exposing flesh. He touches the edges of the open wound with his fingertips.

- He had a bottle. I didn't see it. It's gonna need stitches

- How many times, Noah? You can't run your mouth! You're not your brother.

Noah turns the tap. The jet of water dilutes the blood sending swirls down the black hole.

- Noah. We gotta go, now! He wouldn't stop.

Noah turns to look at the man. The dark butterfly of blood covers his chest

- Course he wouldn't.

SATURDAY.
EXT. PUB GARDEN. EARLY EVENING.

A thin stream of smoke rises towards the streetlight. Dominic leans against the outside wall staring out as he smokes.
The old door swings open. Noah pulls up his hood.

- Well this is fun
- What? You wanna go?
- I never wanted to come in the first place. Let's have twos on that.

Dominic holds out the half-finished cigarette.

- Is that what they're always like?

Noah inhales deeply.

- Every time.

He blows a thick stream of smoke upwards.

- At least they're consistent. I'll give em that. You just gotta hold your own, Dom.

Dominic looks at Noah.

- It's them in that story isn't it? The one on the radio? They're the pub mates.

Noah takes a long drag.

- You put them in the story. Didn't you?

Noah flicks the finished cigarette and looks at Dominic.

- I dunno what you mean. You pissed?

A trickle of rainwater falls from the end of the guttering. Dominic smiles.

- I knew it.

Noah pulls open the old door. Light from inside the pub washes his face. We hear a man's laugh.
Noah steps inside.

INT. BUSY PUB. EVENING.

Old men lean against the old oak of the bar like they're pretending to push it. A young man wearing a full tracksuit and baseball cap feeds pound coins into a slot, hypnotiSed by the dancing rainbow colours of the fruit machine. The faded floral walls hold sepia pictures of the local area a hundred years ago. Small circular tables carry conversations between generations of the same family. The creamy froth of half finished Guinness clings to the inside of glasses. A young woman weaves between dark coats of people collecting finished drinks and out of date compliments.
Dominic moves to the bar fishing coins from his wallet. The young woman lays her hand on his shoulder steering herself from his path. Dominic looks up. The woman smiles.
Through crackled speakers we hear the opening cords of 'Let me be your Fantasy' by Baby D.
The old men at the bar turn towards the jukebox frowning in unison. A large man with a square face and medicine ball stomach puts one hand in the air.

- Tune!

He looks towards a table by the toilet. A group of men look up from their drinks. We see Noah lower his pint class.

- Remember this lads? Q Club? I'll take you hiiiiiiiigheeeeeer!

The men at the table start to laugh. Noah stares out.

VOICE OVER:

It's like finding a fiver, the glow of a crumpled note when you've been scratching around for coins. Whenever the train leaves Coventry and I know there's only twenty more minutes I feel it in my stomach. I find a fiver. My heavy pockets full of coppers get ripped off. I put on my coat. Imagine the station. The escalator up into the Pallasades. The red and white of footlocker. A fiver. Mine to spend. Then as I breathe out, down the ramp into town, the feeling in my stomach changes. No matter how long it's been. A fiver. Could've been a tenner.

SUNDAY.
INT. UPSTAIRS LANDING. MORNING.

Dominic steps out of his bedroom yawning, rubbing his nest of scruffy hair. As he reaches the bathroom we see the other bedroom door is open. Morning light fills the bedroom. Noah sits on the floor between the two beds, his back against the radiator, wearing black bottoms and an old grey vest.

Scattered around him we see about twenty notebooks of different sizes and colours. The ones that are open hold pages filled with scribbled writing.
Noah holds an old blue exercise book in his hands.
Dominic sniffs.

- They're mine.
- What?
- Them bottoms. They're mine.
- Mom put them on my bed.
- Well, they're mine.
- You want them back? I've got no pants on.

Dominic leans in the doorway, one hand down the front of his baggy jogging bottoms.

- Keep em. What you doing?

Noah looks down at the old blue book in his hands.

VOICE OVER:

I come from a place of talkers. Storytellers.
People who pull you in and take you with em.
My brother's explicit descriptions of fingering girls long before I'd even kissed one.
Uncle Lenny talking about walking into a National Front pub

in Northfield with a machete going up to the bar laying the blade down and calmly ordering a white rum.

Granddad telling us about getting broom handle beatings with nine younger brothers just for stealing pumpkin seeds.

Nan cooking breakfast reminiscing over her shoulder about some German priest offering to renounce the church and proposing to her on the boat over.

Surrounded by all these characters every day I swam in a soup of stories. Soaking up every detail. Logging every image. Saving them to speak.

But I never knew a writer, they didn't exist.

- Noah? Noah Moran? It is you. Shit!

INT. SUPERMARKET. LATE MORNING.

A tall slim man in dark blue trousers and shirt stands arms length from Noah. His dark hair is neatly styled, shiny in the white light. His staff badge glints beneath his long shaving-bumped neck.

- Bloody hell! Long time no see Noah. It's me!
- Hello John.
- What you doing?
- I'm shopping.

Noah starts down the cereal aisle. The man skips after him.

- I mean what you doing back again? Miss us did ya?

Noah looks back up the aisle.

- Yeah. I missed you John.
- You looking for something? What you up to these days?
- Oh you know.
- Noah Moran. Shit! How long you back?
- I don't know.

They walk past the busy bakery counter.

- Seems like ages Noah. Shit!
- You like that word don't you.
- I heard you were singing or something. In London?
- Not quite.
- Are you in a band?
- No. I'm not in a band.
- But you sing?
- No John I don't sing.
- So what do you do?

Noah turns on his heels and starts back the way they came. John follows.

- I'm still at this place.
- I can see.

John taps his badge

- Yep. Manager now
- Well done
- Have you seen anyone else? We should go for a drink. There's a couple of new places in town. Shit, Noah, it's good to see ya!
- You too John.

They turn down the tinned aisle. An elderly lady holds a can in each hand.

- Excuse me young man.

They both ignore her. John puffs up his chest

- Yep. Gonna push for regional manager next year I reckon. That's the real money. Nothing like you though eh, Noah? I bet it's all wild parties and dirty girls. Yeah? That's what it's like down there right?
- Apparently
- Expensive though eh? £5 a pint I heard
- Tell you the truth John, I don't really drink now

John laughs.

- Same old Noah. Still taking the piss.

They reach the freezers. Noah sighs. John shakes his head.

- She's not here Noah. She doesn't start til four. Till number nine.

EXT. PLAYGROUND. EARLY AFTERNOON.

The chipped matt metal of the monkey bars holds old black marker graffiti. Noah traces the scribbled letter with his finger. We move out to see him sitting on top of the climbing frame, his hood pulled up, his feet hanging five feet from the ground. Dirty cotton clouds hide the afternoon sun.
An old man with a long face walks through the park gate holding a telescopic lead. He walks at least ten paces before a old Jack Russell waddles through after him, the lead tugging on its neck.
Twenty feet away a teenage boy pushes a girl on the only swing not tied in a knot.
Noah watches them. The girl laughs over her shoulder as the boy fakes to tickle her each time she swings back.
We hear a memory as Noah watches.

- I'm not doing it. Come here.
- Nothing's happening til you do it.
- You serious?
- I'm deadly serious.
- Eve it's not that funny. Come on it's freezing.

- Get off Noah, not til you do it
- I'm not some kind of performing monkey
- Yes you are. If you want this
- You've built it up now. Eve people walk their dogs, I've got my pants off, hurry up!
- Do the voice
- Alright. Give me a sec. Stop laughing
- Say it
(beat)
- I need your clothes, your boots and your motorcycle
- Louder. Like you mean it

EXT. HIGH STREET. AFTERNOON.

Eve steps off the bus. She moves to the side as an older woman carrying a red-faced boy moves past.

- Thanks. He's not helping me today are you?

Eve smiles. From across the street we see her turn up her collar. Noah steps off the kirb. A car beeps its horn. He freezes. Eve looks round. Their eyes meet. From inside the car we see him look at her. She stares back. The car beeps again.

- Make up your mind!

From inside we see her walk towards him in the middle of the road. They stand arms length apart. We watch her mouth move as she stares at him. He doesn't move. His eyes fixed on her. The car beeps again. She turns and walks away.

VOICE OVER:

It's the little things you notice. The way our first response is to not believe something good. Just in case. Scratching the silver off a piece of card with a penny and seeing three fifty pound signs we look over our shoulder expecting someone to step out of the bushes laughing carrying a camera. Concrete shoes hold feet on the ground. A flat cap keeps a level head. You are what you do and you do what you should til it's done. Land locked we sit firm on what makes sense and our rubbish dump seagulls have never seen the sea.

We hear the afternoon bar code symphony.

INT. SUPERMARKET. LATE AFTERNOON

Eve stares across at the next till. The back of a woman twice her age moves a loaf of sliced white bread across the glass scanner. Beyond her the back of another middle-aged woman does the same.
A shadow moves across her face. She pushes the button to operate the conveyer belt.

- Anywhere nice?

A thickset woman in her early fifties, wearing an beige anorak takes out a purse. Her round face full of smile.

- You were away with the fairies, sweetheart. Go anywhere nice?

Eve scans a value pack of PG tips and smiles.

- I didn't go anywhere

MONDAY.
EXT. BUS STOP. EARLY EVENING.

Half a chiseled Hollywood smile beams out from a torn film poster. Noah stands staring across the street at the high red brick walls of the building opposite, topped by shaped metal, lined with barbed wire.
He holds the old blue exercise book in his hand.
An old man sits on the moulded plastic bench to his right in a long sheepskin coat.
Silence.
We see words appear at the bottom of the screen

Subtitles: Been here long? Has the 11 been?

Noah stares across the street. The old man's eyes follow his.

Subtitles: Now there's a place you don't want to be

Noah looks down at the old man. His weathered face sketched with broken blood vessels. He brings a thin cigarette to his lips

Subtitles: Nothing good comes out of there. Trust me son

We see a perfectly formed smoke ring widen as it rises.

Subtitles: Nothing but sad stories

The streetlight nearest them flickers on. Noah turns to face the old man. Their eyes meet.

- Not all of them. Your bus is here

As the bus approaches and the old man boards, Noah stares across at the prison. We hear a conversation as we watch him.

- I should've gone sooner
- He said he didn't want us there. Mom either. How did he look?
- He looked tired
- Is he alright?

- He's in prison, Dom
- I know, I just..what did he say?
- He said you can have the weights
- What? His weights?
- Yeah
- Does that mean you're gonna leave again now?
(beat)
- No
- What you gonna do?
- I'm gonna write a film
- A film? What about?
- About home
- A film about home? What do you mean?
- I mean I'm gonna write a film about home, about here, about Brum. - Will I be in it?
- I would've thought so mate
- It's not gonna be one of them slow ones is it?
- What do you mean?
- I mean them slow ones that you like, all that staring out of the window and voice overs and that
- Shut up
- Put guns in it
- Guns?
- Yeah, guns. Blow some stuff up. And a car chase, and a proper fight, and a tripping out scene, and boobs. You should start with a murder
- A murder?

- Yeah, that way it's proper gripping from the beginning, like Columbo
- I'm not a detective Dom, look I want it to be real. I want it to be about Birmingham, what it means
(beat)
- Sounds rubbish
- Forget I said anything
- I'm joking Noah. So how will it start
- I dunno

AERIAL SHOT.
A PATCHWORK OF DIFFERENT GREYS DOTTED WITH THE AMBER OF STREETLIGHTS. ZOOM IN. THE SINGLE DECKER BUS ROLLS ALONG THE STREET LIGHTING A SECTION OF PAVEMENT AT A TIME WITH THE GLOW FROM ITS WINDOWS. WE MOVE IN UNTIL WE ARE ALONGSIDE AT WINDOW HEIGHT. THE BUS IS EMPTY EXCEPT FOR AT THE BACK A MAN IN HIS LATE TWENTIES SITS LEANING AGAINST THE WINDOW, HIS GREY HOOD PULLED UP UNDER A BROWN JACKET. HIS HEAD DOWN, HE SCRIBBLES INTO AN OLD BLUE EXERCISE BOOK

VOICE OVER:

I grew up late. Didn't have a clue what I wanted to do and blamed it on a place.

Bored out of my mind til I was 25 I turned on home and left.
Didn't look back.

Fuck you I'm off write stories.

It was in them all. Everything I wrote came out soaked in home.

Every little detail I couldn't see when I was there jumped up and bit me in the face when I left.

I saw where I was from and fell in love.

TUESDAY.
INT. EMPTY KITCHEN. MORNING.

Dominic walks in yawning.

He scratches his stomach through his old white vest. The shaded sideboard catches sunlight through the open blinds. From behind Dominic we see through the window Noah stands in the back garden on the short path of broken slabs. His grey hoody pulled up, he breathes into cupped hands. Dominic clicks the kettle on and stands back from the window, staring out.

EXT. GARDEN.

From the floor we look up at Noah. Something catches his eye. We see him drag an old dirty white football from the edge of the grass with his right foot. He lowers his hands and we see him smile.

In one movement he brings the ball under control rolls it back and flicks it up over his head, spinning round in time to kill it dead on the top of his foot. He stands motionless, arms out, the ball balanced calmly between his laces and toes.

INT. KITCHEN.

Dominic steps forward and smiles.

- Sick

'RETURN'

Old Me
(2011)

produced by Roundhouse
directed by Leo Kay
script development by Yael Shavit
design by Marie Blunck
lighting design by Cis O'Boyle
sound design & musical score by Daniel Clark

Kneeling
on the thin bedroom carpet
in my school shirt and trousers and an old black tie,
face pressed against the glass, watching uncle Joe and another man take turns to fully punch each other in the face.
I'm 10. It's my first proper funeral.
It's almost like they're dancing. Both of them stood, in their cheap suits, down on the patchy back lawn, crunching their fists into each other's faces. One punch at a time.
Nan and Mom and a bunch of cousins I've never met before are all down stairs, crammed into the living room around a dead body.
I can hear Louis Armstrong's 'We have all the time in the World'.

Each one punches, then waits and takes one. Like a conversation.

Less than an hour later I'm sitting in the kitchen watching them two, sat in the corner, laughing.
Turns out they're brothers. Two brothers sat laughing and swigging cans through split lips on purple mouths, spitting out stories of schoolboy beatings, their eyes swollen shut, hands like bags of broken stone.

The honour of animals.
The spark in my gut.
I can't help it. It's genes. I'm predisposed.
Predisposed to the romance of a broken nose.

MONDAY

Morning playground.
I stand statue, while you and your friend Jonah giggle like hyenas and soak my crotch with a trickling hose. The cold air's cutting through my soaked jeans to the skin of my thighs.
Parents and kids wait for the morning bell.
- Oh oh. I think it's happening again boys. I can feel it. Lightning, shooting from my bum! Purple Lightning! Catch it!
You and Jonah chase me, laughing so hard you snort.
A man in dark clothes walks over. We stop.
He's late thirties and takes care of himself, all clean lines and cotton, like some kind of Muji prison officer.
He looks at me. Then my crotch. Then at me again and pulls the kind of face that Gorillas pull when someone comes to make a documentary.
As Jonah is led away frowning, I pull my best Gorilla face. Jonah laughs. His Muji dad turns round. The bell goes.
Stare off. *You don't know me mate.*
- Right big man, got everything? Lunch box? Check. P.E Kit? Check.

Good, gimme a kiss, now get inside, and have fun yeah?

I throw up into the Sainsbury's carrier bag.
My dark puke full of bile. My ribs hurt.
Andy leans the sheet of plasterboard against the wooden frame we built yesterday.
Chris Moyles talks over the start of a song we've heard twice already this morning.
I can taste the cement powder.
- I wish he'd shut up.
I wretch again. Stabbing pain in my ribs.
Andy shakes his head.
- What're you like? I told you you should've left when I did, them lot were nuts, I swear that one guy had a kid, you even know what you were on?
As he carries on talking I get a flash of strangers laughing, an empty bottle of Tequila on a grubby coffee table, a dirty white tiger and me bent over with a rolled up twenty pound note.
- What happened?
- Same thing that always happens. We argued, she wants me to move down there
- So why don't you go?
- Cos it's not that simple is it? So what, I move down there, get some shitty job and scrape to get by?
- Yeah. If you wanna be with her

- And then what? End up slowly hating it, blaming her and it all turns to shit, and I'm stuck in London? I'm alright thanks.

I pull my pen out of my pocket and scribble onto a torn piece of battered sandpaper.
Know your limits (projected hand written)

Chris Moyles cracks another shit joke over the end of the song to sign off his shift. I hold up the plasterboard sheet as Andy nail guns it to the frame.
My stomach feels like it's been scraped out with a fork.
We stand back to admire our work. the long room is one big off-white plasterboard canvas.
I wretch again.
- What're you like? You should write a rhyme about it. We'll make a track. We'll call it Know your limits.

We're in the bank.
Your little brother's clinging onto my side like a koala. Your mom's outside on the phone.
The woman behind the plexi-glass window looks like someone. Who does she look like?
She looks at your brother and smiles. He buries his face into my neck playing shy.
She asks him if he's having fun with Daddy and I wonder whether she expects a 1 yr old to answer. The cash drawer's open.

I stare at the packed notes. She notices me staring at the money and pushes it closed. Davros.
Leader of the Daleks. Woman looks just like Davros.
- Would you like me to get one of our advisors to call you to discuss your financial options?
- My financial options?
And just like that I think of me and Andy, 17 years old, putting on shirts and ties and going into the Halifax in town sitting opposite the bank guy, grilling him.
- Yeah I'm gonna need a piggy bank shaped like a wild animal yeah?
- I'm gonna need my nickname on my chequebook
- How much interest would I get a week on one million?
- Forty pounds.
- Excuse me?
- Forty pounds.
Davros slides my card back through the little opening and smiles as she tells me I'm forty pounds away from my overdraft limit.

I remember looking up at nan.
Her face is calm despite the size of the gingham shopping bags in each of her hands. I can see the muscles near her elbow, under the skin. Like a race horse.
I'm struggling alongside her with a family size box of Persil,

torn between using my hip as a mobile shelf, the old school
bear-hug carry and balancing it on my 8-yr-old shoulder.
Her eyes look straight ahead, but I know she sees me.
I need her to know I can do this. I don't need help.
We're half a mile from home.

The year 9 boy stares at me. Like he's convinced the answer is
hidden in my face. His eyes twitch. I can almost hear his
brain working.
His mate digs his arm and tells him to forget it, that nothing
rhymes with orange.
I smile. He refuses to give up. Their young teacher shouts over
that we need to finish our pieces and not to worry about
the rhyme.
While the rest of the class get on with their work I lean on the
boy's table and tell him that if he wants to take the whole session's time trying to rhyme orange, I'm alright with that and to
make sure he shows me what he comes up with.
His mate asks me if I've noticed how when I'm just speaking out
loud normally it's like I'm rhyming, a few others agree.
I smile and tell him I don't know what he's talking about but
how sometimes, when I'm just walking about, a thought will
come out and before I know what I'm doing I'm sorting it out,
into a pattern to the point where nothing else matters, even
when I'm crossing the road and about to flattened by a bus,

I can't rush an idea and I know that might sound like I'm quite weird, but maybe it's kinda like when a drummer stands in the queue at the bank and without even knowing starts tapping a beat with his hand and his feet and the other people notice and start to focus on the rhythm and that there are so many patterns in the way that we speak in the cadence and spaces between, how we breathe, our intonation not to mention emphasis and the gentle inflective differences cos everyone of us has our own way of speaking that carries a unique way of reaching out to other people and if that's what he means?

- I dunno, sir. I just thought you were rappin, ennit?

Andy turns off the engine. I look up at Mom's house.
The small window top right is mine.
He hands me a torn piece of battered sandpaper covered in words.
- You should get yourself a notebook. If you're taking it seriously now, you need a notebook.
He lights a cigarette. I rub my thumb across the jagged paper.
My hands are rough.
He starts the engine.
- See you tomorrow, we've gotta smash up that old shed and knock down them walls.
I squeeze the sandpaper in my hand as his Volkswagen pulls away. _____

When we were nine, we used to make up kung-fu dance routines in the back garden to impress the girl next door but one. Sam.

I don't remember her surname. She was about 4 or 5 years older than us and obviously gorgeous. We'd make a den out of an old terry towelling sheet, get inside, strip down to our pants and plan our moves.

The buzz before we jumped out to perform.

- What moves are ya gonna do?
- I dunno. What moves are you gonna do?
- I dunno. Don't copy me.
- I'm not gonna copy ya. What are ya gonna do?
- I dunno. Just do anything. But make it good.
- How old is she?
- 14 I think.
- 14?
- I know, that's why we've gotta be cool.
- What if she laughs?
- She won't laugh. Why would she laugh?
- What if she does? Why do we have to be in just our pants?
- Shut up. Look if she laughs we tell her to eat shit and mud bomb her house later, yeah?
- Yeah
- Right, come on
- I'm cold.
- Me too, but we're doing it

- Are they my Hulk pants?
- What?
- You're wearing my hulk pants.
- I'm not.
- You can't wear my pants
- Look are we going? She's waiting
- I want em back
- Forget the Hulk pants! I just wanted to wear good ones.
- Yeah and now I look boring. I could've worn the Spiderman ones.
- It doesn't matter. Just impress her with your moves.
- I haven't got any moves!
- Ssshhh! Don't worry, just copy me.

There's a little part of me. Not massive, but it's there, that believes that if you've never even had the thought of having someone's name tattooed on your body, like, just the thought, you don't really love them.

We're in the kitchen.

My phone vibrates against the small lacquered table top for the umpteenth time.

I watch you thinking as you spear individual pieces of sweetcorn onto each prong of your fork. I can feel your

brain working.
Your mom and your brother are in the other room watching cartoons. I sip my tea. My phone vibrates again. I glance at the missed calls symbol on my phone and ask you how school was. You hold up your fork and tell me it looks like a crown for a mouse.

Don't ever seem too happy lad.
Don't ever let it get to a point where you're the kind of person who people think of as happy.
He's always in a good mood isn't he? Pleasure to be around.
Don't be that person. Let yourself have moments, but keep em under wraps. Don't be throwing that out on the world.
When you go around like that, that's when you get hit by a bus. That's when you wake up with cancer. You never hear about a miserable old bastard getting cancer. You never hear people saying,
Yeah he was a shit every second of his life, I'm glad the bus hit him.
There's no loss in that. No tragedy.
And if there's one thing we know, it's that God loves a tragedy.

Feel it on my tongue.

Like licking a battery.

- Wait. Don't go yet. Let it hit your throat. Swallow.

- You good?

I can feel my blood.

Stomach jumps.

- Close your eyes.

- Right, together 5, 4, 3, 2

- Run!

Arms out. Down the slope. Faster. Soft grass under my feet.

- Run!

Feel the air in my face, running over my cheeks round into my ears

Open eyes. Dark sky. Blurred edges. Moonlight. Faster. Breath deep. Take it in.

- You got anything?

- Not yet

Running

- I've got something

- What?

- Purple lightning

- Where?

- Purple Lightning!

- I see it!

Light between steps. Like a gazelle

- The trees

- Look at the trees! You see that?

The trees are running. Roots for legs.

- The Trees are Running!

Full gallop.

Longer strides.

Hang in the air. Like the BFG. I'm the BFG.

- We're fucking BFGs!

Together.

Over the brook, still flat out.

Racehorses.

Up at the sky.

- Look at the moon. The moon's massive!

- Massive moon!

He howls. I howl.

- AAAOoooooooooooooooooow!

We're wolves.

Running. Look at my hands. Hair. Thriller. Thriller hands.

- Thriller hands!

Together.

Feel my bones.

Lungs burn.

Pace slows. Up the slope. Silver grass.

Breathe deep.

Heavy feet.

Spinning head. Pirouette.

Fall back.

Curved black. Massive moon. Perfect. We're inside a snow dome.

- We're in a snow dome.

Laughing.
Together.
Together.

TUESDAY

I'm a rhino.
We're in the baby gym.
Your brother's hiding behind a big purple pregnancy ball wetting himself laughing. I start my charge, your brother bolts for it, his little legs rocking from side to side, speed wobbling away, screaming in excitement.
A hoola hoop hits me and rattles onto it's side. Two big feet.
Expensive pastel socks.
Muji Dad.
A little girl about your brother's age comes up and hides behind his legs, hugging his thigh.
A nod.
Your brother runs over and crashes into me. I tackle him to the floor. Muji Dad picks up the hoola hoop and hands it to his little girl like it's hers.
Your brother points.
- Hoop. Girl.
- That's right. The girl has the hoop. Good boy.
They don't move.
Awkward silence.
His Blackberry rings and he swivels round to answer it. Relief.

His little girl is left facing me and your brother.
She stares us, gripping the hoola hoop tight to her chest.
- Hello. What's your name? Wow, ok, hello Morris. Have you got the hoola hoop?
What girls name sounds like Morris?
Morris looks at your brother. Your brother looks at her. Sparks fly. They run off, leaving me on my knees, eyes level with Muji Dad's arse.

Nan used to say the best ducks can swim in any pond. If you're good with the fact that you're a duck you don't have to try and be a swan and you don't need to pretend you're better when you're swimming with the pigeons.
Do pigeons even swim?
It's funny how there's some people you just don't ever question.

Two sledge hammers rest against the outside of the house.
My hands are hot. Where there was a concrete shed and three walls, now there's just a blanket of rubble.
- I love smashing stuff.
Andy swigs from his tea.
- Everybody loves smashing stuff.
I feel the muscles in my back as I fill my lungs with smoke.
He tells me I still smoke like a 12 year old girl.

- You still watching school girls smoke then?
- You're a funny guy.
I look at him.
- What you mean the way I talk?
He takes his cue.
- No, I'm just saying, you know, the way you tell the story
I play Anthony's role too.
- Tommy no, You got it all wrong. Oh, Anthony. He's a big boy, he knows what he said. What did ya say? Funny how?
- Just... ya know... you're funny.
- You mean, let me understand this cause, ya know maybe it's me, I'm a little fucked up maybe, but I'm funny how, I mean funny like I'm a clown, I amuse you?

We used to trip in the woods.
Two seventeen year olds looking for more.
Andy knew a student guy who made his own acid. We'd sit, split a little bottle of Kiwi 20/20, reminisce and take the piss out of each other until we we're properly laughing. That was the rule. You don't take anything until we're laughing. Together.
Tab each. Drop it and run. Bomb it down the big dip and up the other side.
The whole game was to shout whatever you saw and get the other person to see it. Anything you could think of.
Crazy stuff. _____

A massive fake fish.

Bug eyes staring out. Rubber mouth carved into a smile.

You'd have given him a name by now. You'd love this place.

Optical illusion coffee table, fake tree standing lamp.

I sink into the deep leather sofa. The girl at the reception desk dressed as Tarzan's Jane stares at me.

- We're so glad you could come in for a chat. We love your work. Love it.

My stomach feels empty. Just be cool. Listen to everything before you say anything stupid. This could be important.

In front of me the back end of a fibre glass plane sticks out as though it has crashed into the wall. Jane starts telling me about how her boyfriend likes her better with a full body tan and how expensive it is to maintain a consistent colour.

Just be cool.

Duran Duran starts to play through self aware speakers and I think about the school disco when me and Andy wore matching chinos and shirts and I danced with Tracey Cunnane because she was the only girl without a partner and I felt bad for her and how she wouldn't let go when the song finished and how everyone was watching and starting to laugh and I tried to get away but she wouldn't let go and how as Rick Astley started I pushed her over and ran off leaving her crying on the floor.

Tarzan's Jane tells me he's ready for me and points to a spiral staircase. _____

It's not a steady build up. It's not more and more pebbles being added to the scale until it tips. It's not accumulation.
But it's not instinct. It's not the body acting before the brain is engaged. It's something else.

He looks like someone. Who does he look like?
My stomach turns. I think of you and your brother. Stay cool. There's more than just you to think about now.
- A comedian?
- Don't get me wrong, you're clever. You're not your standard punchline type. You don't think you're a comedian?
My hands twitch.
 - Not really.
He leans forward. Elbows on his deep ergonomic desk. Who does he look like?
- Oh. I'm sorry, I thought I was talking to someone who might want to earn 10 grand a week
What did he say? Did he just say? Roy Scheider. From Jaws. Geezer looks just like Roy Schieder from Jaws.
- Sorry?
- Not straight away obviously. I'm talking post Edinburgh run, when a series was up and running.
Series? What's he talking about? 10 grand? Comedian?
Stay cool. Think. Look at him. Smug bastard. He knows I'm squirming.
10 grand a week? What's that a year?

- Yeah. Edinburgh run, then we pitch a series. I'm assuming you've got ideas for a series yeah?

What the fuck's he talking about? He's talking about 10 grand a week. Look at him. He's loving this. Be cool. Look at his face. Roy Scheider. Stop it. No, fuck him. Dangling his carrot, his 'still down with the kids' G-Shock watch. His little office at the top of the spiral staircase like he's some kinda of all powerful fucking money wizard. Ooooh ten grand a week, Fuck him. Stop it.
Think.

- I think first thing to do would be to have you write something for this pilot we're working on. Something small, but funny. We're having a meeting this Friday so it'll need to be done by then. You think you can do that?

That's 520 grand a year. *Tell him to shove it.* Will you shut up? He's waiting.

- Yeah. Small and funny. Yep, I can do that

You've changed.
Everybody's heard that. Was a time when that was the worst thing you could hear. Like the aim of it all was staying the same. Like the worst thing you could do was not be what you were. _____

We're sitting at a long table, waiting for food we don't remember ordering. I'm scanning people trying to put names to faces. I saw something somewhere where they said when you meet someone new you should make sure to say their name back to them, as you shake hands.
- "Nigel? nice to meet you Nigel"
I never do it.
10 grand a week. (projected in courier font)
I reach for your hand on the table, you spread your fingers without looking, letting me slot mine into the spaces as you carry on a conversation with a guy who looks a bit like your ex boyfriend and I wonder if you've noticed.
I think about the fact I've got a gig later and wish I could just stay with you and, as a short waiter lowers tapas onto the table, I remember you saying we should take more photos of the boys.
When my Mom and Dad first split up, I remember playing it cool.
A few of my mates had parents who were divorced and I was drilling myself with the two christmases and two birthdays angle.
I started refusing to be in photographs. Proper little arse I was. I'd run off or hide my head in my top.
After a while people gave up trying, which is why, to this day if all you had to go on was family photo albums, you'd think I died in 1992.

Everybody's agreeing how much they enjoy tapas.

I'm thinking I'd rather just have one big plate to myself.
How if food was to share they'd call it something else.
How I was 21 before I learned to eat with my elbows down. In our house if you finished last, people thought you didn't want it.
I think about the time Andy came over after school and we got fish and chips and all of us sat on the floor in front of the telly and at one point Andy went to the toilet and when he came back his chips were gone.
10 grand a week. (In courier font)
We're the youngest couple here by at least five years and I know we're the only ones who don't have a dining room. We're the only ones who don't even have room for a sofa.
The guy who looks like your ex boyfriend says that Bali was incredible and asks you where we're thinking of going on holiday this year and you look at me sheepishly and tell him we haven't decided yet and for a second I hate you. Then I hate me.
That's 520 grand a year. (in courier font)
My stomach tightens. You notice.
You give me that look that says that now is not the time and can we please just enjoy dinner and your eyes beat me and I smile.
I think of my granddad. Making jokes when things were at their worst. Him telling us that if you can't laugh then you've lost and that our family doesn't lose.
I think of him getting me to choose horses for him and kiss the betting slips. I remember sipping my dandelion and burdock through a coloured straw, sitting silently in the afternoon pub as he stared up at the horses on the little TV screen. The skin on

the back of his hands as he gripped his pint glass, like tissue paper over a road map of blue vessels and as everyone else starts to order dessert I squeeze your hand and ask for a Guinness.

I'm holding an unlit roly.
The thin man next to me tells me he enjoyed my set.
Outside the bar is busy, people stood drinking, spilling into the road.
- Thanks
He's about my age, but slightly taller.
He tells me I should think about TV. That my style would work on TV. I don't ask him what he means.
- You need a plan. You need to work out what your chasing, make a plan and stick to it. That's the only way you'll make it doing this.
I squeeze the roly in my fingers.
- Where do you see yourself in 5 years?
And just like that it's Christmas eve. I'm 19, stood in a working mens club back home next to Chris Northall. He's going on about how a degree was pointless. How he'll have a house before I even finish uni. How I'm wasting my time just digging myself into debt. For some reason I'm holding my pint at the top. My grip tightening as he goes on and on.
- You want my advice?

The smug look at his face.

And how it changed when he saw my blood.

A man with a long beard and trucker cap walks over and holds out two bottles of expensive cider, smiling. He asks what we're talking about.

- I was just telling this guy what he needs to be doing

People'll watch you. Trying to find something. A chink in your armour. A fault in your stitching. It's just what they're like.

They need to know you've got weakness.

It doesn't matter.

The time they spend trying to find something to pick at will be wasted if you already know.

Nobody's perfect, but your faults are yours.

Nobody else gets to own em

- You see your problem yeah-

- I know

- But, I'm telling you you're problem-

- Yeah, I know and it doesn't really matter does it. You finished?

And just like that they're on their back. Little legs peddling thin air because the only weapon they had is useless.

People will always watch you lad.

You just watch yourself.

WEDNESDAY

Eyes open. Blurry.
Rain soaked glass.
Dry throat. The edges of a person. My Dad.
My body's numb, still morphined up.
My wrist bandaged, arm strapped over my head in traction. It's Christmas day. I'm 19.
Artificial light.
His edges becoming solid. He's shaking his head.
Must've been nearly three years since I'd even seen him at that point. He looked well. Younger somehow. Like time had been good to him.
He's smiling. Shaking his head and smiling.
"What're you like?"

I watch you on the climbing frame. Weighing up the fireman's pole. You're not sure. It's pretty high.
Other kids are going crazy, swarming over the slide and rope net like ants. Parents line up by the door waiting for the morning bell. Muji Dad is on his phone.
Jonah steams up the slide and tries to push past you to the pole. You hold your ground. Go on lad.
Jonah pushes again. You don't budge. Jonah shoves you hard

and you fall forward. My stomach turns. You try to grip the pole but miss and fall forward. I'm running.

You sit crying on the sponged floor. You're elbow's grazed, but you're ok. Jonah stands looking down, shocked.

I can feel my blood.

Muji Dad walks over, finishing his conversation like it's a real pain.

- Yeah, look I'm gonna have to go. It's just my kid.

I pick you up.

Jonah looks worried. Muji Dad smiles and ruffles his hair.

- No harm done.

- What?

The bell goes.

You wipe your face and give me a hug. I can feel my blood.

As you and Jonah go inside Muji Dad shrugs. I look at his throat.

- Boys eh? Sometimes you've just gotta leave them to it haven't you?

- That's easy to say when it's your kid doing the pushing.

He looks at me.

I look at him.

And suddenly the playground is empty.

Slow rolling drums.

He steps away to the left, slowly unbuttoning his shirt. I step away to the right, slowly pulling my arms out of my t-shirt.

Cut to a tiny kitten on a nearby roof as it stares at two men taking off their tops in a playground.

Muji Dad is now topless. His chest rug is dense, spreading into alban shoulder wings of hair, perfectly symetrical.

I am less hairy on the chest but my shoulder tattoo somehow balances out the machismo.

The tiny kitten watches as the two men warm up, keeping their distance from each other.

Muji Dad cracks his knuckles. I crack my knuckles.

He throws air punches. Snapping his elbow. I do the same.

The tiny kitten tilts his head.

I fan my fingers and ball fists. My eyes narrow. A nod. Then-

---

I line up the ball.

Resting it on the flattened coke bottle.

Andy stands on the other side of the room in the goal we drew onto the plasterboard in thick pencil. He's giving it the Bruce Grobbelaar wobbly legs trying to put me off. Cigarette hanging from his lips.

And I picture you in a café, reading, thin roly between your fingers, strands of your hair failing across your face.

You, engrossed in your book, waiting until you finish your page to stroke it back behind your ear. How that action's yours. And will be forever.

- What you smiling about Dicksplash?
- Dicksplash?
- Did you phone her?
- What?

- Just take the frigging shot.
I look towards the top right corner.
- You think I'm stupid? Don't try and fool with with your eyes, just shoot.
I fan my fingers and squeeze tight fists with both hands. My eyes narrow.
- Who'd you think you are? Bruce Lee?
Chris Moyles says something unfunny. Andy smiles. I take one step and

---

stare at the blank word document. The cafe's quiet.
Outside in the street, men are throwing rubbish into the back off a truck.
On the chair next to me a large white tiger sits motionless. It's fur grubby from children's fingers. It's moulded eyes staring at the screen. I run my fingers over the plastic laptop keys.
My hands are smooth.
- Small and funny. I can do that right?
The tiger stares out.
Outside one of the men curses as a bin bag tears spilling it's rotting guts all over him and the floor.
I type 10 grand a week (projected courier font types) at the top of the screen in large font.
I look at the tiger.
fuck him (projected in speech bubble)

- What?

The tiger stares out.

- Small and funny. Come on.

Outside, the rubbish truck pulls away leaving just a flattened bottle of coke in the road.

He had these boots. Light tan leather, just above the ankle. Not quite cowboy boots, more like work shoes that you could just wear. I don't remember what happened, I mean, I don't remember why I did it. I was 4. I've told myself he must've said or done something, but I honestly don't remember what. Anyway, I pissed in one. I zipped up the zip on the side so it would spill, knelt down next to it and pissed. Nobody else was in the room.

I remember the sound.

That's nuts right?

I mean why would you do that?

Why would you piss in your dad's shoes?

We collapse on the floor laughing.

Your head rests on my outstretched arm. In profile you look like Charlie Brown. Your cheeks are flushed. I push your nose like a button. You reach out and touch my mouth and ask me why

my top lip has a little extra bit in the middle.
I tell you I got it from my dad.
- Your dad?
I can feel your brain working. You feel your top lip with your finger. You've got your mom's mouth.
I prepare myself for a big question. I want to be honest.
The front door opens and, as your little brother shouts up the stairs, you ask me which animal does the biggest poo.

Easter bonnet competition.
I'm 9.
First prize is a cassette walkman. I want one so badly.
The letter from school says 'no adult help'. I've explained to Nan how everyone else will pretty much get their moms to make it and how they'll be amazing and I'll never win.
She made me do it myself. She said knowing I'd done it myself would feel like winning.
I stayed up til ten working on it. Went to sleep with felt and glitter in my hair. It was a cardboard cutout easter bunny dressed like Michael Jackson doing the moonwalk. His little glitter glove. Sugar paper Fedora. The square dance floor formed the top of the hat.
It was shit.
Everyone else got help and there's were amazing. Chris Northall had a full crucifixion scene with a balsa wood cross and a little model Mary and everything and he couldn't even draw a

decent stickman.

He won the cassette walkman.

I came home, rubbish Michael Jackson bunny hanging from my hand.

I went straight to the kitchen to throw it in the bin in front of Nan. But she wasn't there.

The kitchen was empty. And there, on the table, a brand new cassette walkman and a little note that just said, "You did it".

(window projection. rain on glass)

I lie in bed staring at the ceiling.

I lie in bed staring at the ceiling (projected script types)

I know that on the other side of that painted plaster board there is a web of wires bringing power to the tiny circle lights.

I can hear mom's light snore through the thin wall. (projected script types)

I can hear you breathing under the covers in the recovery position.

I can hear the hum of the fish tank filter downstairs.

(projected script type)

On the other side of the partition wall behind my head I know that two boys are asleep in the same pose as you. Three bodies out cold. Like you fell from a building into comfort.

Outside the wind runs it's hand around the house. (projected script types in synch as I say it)
I think about his face. Roy Scheider. His smug smile.
Small and funny.
I think about what Andy said earlier in the car. (projected script type)
10 grand a week. That could set us up.
So go. Move down there. (projected script type)
And do what? Walk onto a building site? Do another shitty office thing while I'm shelling out more?
Yeah. any of them. If you want her. (projected script type)
I look at you, your chin up like a sleeping cat.
I do want her.
So go. do whatever you have to and go. (projected script type)
I stare at the ceiling.
On the other side of that painted plaster there is a web of wires.
I can't.
So shut up about her. Never mention her again. (projected script types in synch as I say it)

Avoid a fight at all costs.
There's nothing to be gained from a fight you could've avoided.
If you punch somebody in the face properly, you're gonna mess up your wrist. Maybe break a knuckle. For what?
Walk away.

The rage in your stomach will pass and the second it starts to subside you'll be washed with the guilt of knowing that what you just did was absolutely pointless.

Nobody wants it. The louder somebody gets, the less likely they are to fight. Volume's a smokescreen for fear. You can see it in a person's eyes.

Walk away.

If you can go through your life without it, you're winning.

People die from punches.

But, if it's on.

And you'll know. You'll feel it.

Deeper than nerves. Thicker than blood. This is unavoidable.

I'm trapped. Even if I turn to leave he's gonna attack.

If you feel that son, you hit first.

You remember where the centre of your body is and you punch.

You punch up and from the middle and you look to hit a couple of inches past where you're aiming and don't go for his face, his face is hard, you want this over.

You remember what I taught you, you breath out and strike as hard as you can and you aim for his throat.

THURSDAY

Eyes open. Wretch.

Skin crawls. Cold. Brain pushes against my skull. Eyes burn. Stomach scraped out with a fork.

Where am I?

Body bent to fit on small mattress.

I'm in a plastic Ferrari.

Massive stuffed tiger staring. Dark eyes. Grubby white fur.

I'm in a kids room.

Jaw aches.

Dry mouth.

Curl up, ease my hands between my legs. Thighs soaked.

Piss.

I've pissed myself.

Skin crawls.

Floor to ceiling mirror.

See me.

Ripped shirt. Dark eyes.

I'm in somebody's little kid's room

Hello?

Speaking

I'm fine thanks. How are you?

No. I haven't checked for bit

Yeah I've got internet banking. I just haven't been on.

Pardon?

How much?

- Hold up big man. Hold on. We're ok. We're not late. Daddy's just on the phone.

Sorry. It's my little boy.

Right and what does that mean?

How much?

A day or every time?

What if more than one thing tries to go out?

Yep.

Yeah, I get it. The thing is I'm waiting on payments, I'm free lance.

A writer. Performer. I teach. It's complicated

No, I know the numbers are straightforward

Yes.

I'm waiting on payment for two jobs that'll cover the difference easily.

Yeah.

I don't know. I've chased them up. It's kind of out of my hands.

One second

- Hey, hold up big man. Don't let go of my hand in the road. We're not late

Yeah I'm here.

What do you mean action?

I understand.

Yeah, and I just said

I'm not raising my voice. You know what.

- On the phone? Well, that was the evil Banko. He was telling me that unless we get to school in the next two minutes he'll destroy the climbing frame and take over the world. You better run ahead and check it out.

Your hand slips out of mine as we mount the curb at the corner. From the other side Muji Dad and Jonah cross heading in the same direction. We stare at them. They stare at us.
Out of nowhere a massive Range Rover cuts round the corner nearly knocking all four of us over. It speeds off without a second thought.
My blood.
You're fine. Jonah's fine.
The pair of you run ahead driving imaginary turbo jeeps.
- Idiot.
- I know. What the hell you need a range rover for anyway, - speed bumps?
- Exactly.
I look at him. He looks at me.
A nod, (slide guitar starts)
We walk side by side in silence, two dads, the morning sun lighting us from behind.

I bring the small piece of yellow paper to my mouth and kiss it, as I find our race amongst the wall of TV screens.
Andy's outside in the car. He couldn't bear to come in and watch.

I look at the names in biro on the back of my hand.//
They're off.//
My stomach's dancing. If our horse doesn't win, the 800 quid we've saved is gone and we can kiss goodbye to our American road trip. If it comes in. We're half way there.//
This was my idea.//
Home straight. Come on. Come on.//
Focking come on!

An old man curses and scrunches up his slip.//
I don't know what to do. I can feel my blood.//
We've now got 1500 quid.//
I wanna scream. *Stay calm. Think. 1500 quid is brilliant, but it's still not enough.*//
Walk out. Walk out right now.//
I look at my hand.//
If I do it once more we'll have enough.//
Stop it. Andy's outside. 1500 quid's amazing.//
I look at my hand.//
Don't be a knob. Think.//
I take a fresh betting slip from the little trough.//
Think!//
Grandma's Hands. 2:15. 2 to 1. To win.

Eyes open.

I'm running

Black sky.

The heat pressing on my chest

Cutting between people.

Almost falling.

Trails of light.

Blurred colours

So hot.

96 degrees at night.

Las Vegas

Feel the booze in my blood

White Russians.

The dude abides

Is that a pyramid?

Cameras are flashing. Cars shouting

So hot.

Need to get to the hotel. Need the pool.

Cool water.

Laughing.

Where's Andy?

Is that a castle?

Need the pool.

That's a castle

Lobby.

Pretty girl on reception. The look on her face.

Straight through

Out onto the patio.

Smell chlorine
I made it. Dark sky
There's the edge.
Water looks perfect
Arms out
Take off..

I remember lying there.
In the bottom of the empty swimming pool in Las Vegas at two in the morning. Unable to move.
Thinking about how far away I was from home.
Thinking about what people back home were doing at that exact moment. How nobody would believe where I was, in fact how everyone would believe it and that being worse.
Andy out on the street looking for me.
Thank fuck it was the shallow end.
My body numb. The stabbing pain in my chest. The white tiles stretching away from my head like hundreds of little blank pages.
I could feel the cold of open wounds. The warmth of concussion. Blood.
It went dark then light then dark again and the last thing I remember is trying to laugh. Like there was nothing else to do.

———————————————

- Ok, big man. One more.

You're face lights up. Your brother is already fast asleep in his cot.

- Ok. So. Once upon a time there were these two squirrels. Yeah, squirrels and their names were, what were their names? You sure? Ok. Nuts and Zoomer.

So Nuts and Zoomer had known each other since they were babies. They grew up together, went to squirrel school together, but they were very different. See, Nuts loved to play and enjoy himself and run around. He loved football and would play all day until he had to go to bed and even then he'd sleep with the football in the bed with him. Yeah, under the covers.

Now Zoomer, was a bit different. He liked to plan. He was always thinking about what was going to happen tomorrow and the next day and the day after that and on and on. Always thinking Zoomer was.

Anyway, it was summer and Nuts was out playing football, enjoying himself when he saw Zoomer digging around in the grass.

What are you doing Zoomer? asked Nuts. That's his voice. Zoomer didn't even look up.

I can't stop to talk now Nuts. I'm busy collecting nuts.

Nuts? said Nuts. But, there's loads of nuts, why do you need to collect them?

Because soon it will be autumn and then winter and there'll be no nuts and what will you do then, eh?

Oh come on Zoomer, come and have a kick around. The sun is shining, look there's some girls watching. Enjoy yourself.

No thank you, said Zoomer. You go on enjoying yourself, but don't come crying to me when it's freezing and the ground is covered in snow and you've got no nuts to eat.

Ok Zoomer, see you later.

And Nuts carried on enjoying himself while Zoomer carried on digging for nuts.

This is getting confusing with the names big man.

Anyway autumn came around, Nuts carried on enjoying himself and Zoomer carried on stocking up his nuts with his head down. Soon enough winter came and the ground grew hard and covered with snow.

It was too cold to play football and there was nothing to eat. Nuts was hungry. He had no food and there was no food to find. He went to Zoomer's place and knocked on the door.

Zoomer opened the door in his smoking jacket, eating a nut burger, sipping a nut juice.

Nuts stood shivering on the doorstep.

Can I help you, Nuts?

Please can I come in and have some of your nuts, Zoomer? I haven't got any and I'm really hungry.

Zoomer smiled.

I warned you didn't I. What did I say? What did I say?

Nuts looked down. You said that if I carried on enjoying myself I'd regret it when winter came, that I should think about the future.

Yes. I did.

And he shut the door in Nuts face. Nuts just stood there,

shivering. He thought to himself, I know there's a lesson to be learned here. I understand that. It just boils my squirrel blood that it has to be taught in such a smug, condescending and self-righteous way. You know what? Zoomer can go fuck himself.

Think about the future? He's sat in there now with his nuts burger and nut juice in the warm, but what else?

He's got no mates cos he never had time for anyone and he hasn't even got any happy memories of fun times to keep him company cos he never had any fun. He's just gonna sit in there, wearing his little smoking jacket, getting fat off nuts and at some point he'll look at his fat squirrel face in his little acorn mirror and realise that all his planning, all his stockpiling nuts and 'I told you so' attitude counts for shit all when you put it in the context of what actually constitutes a full life.

Nuts took out his squirrel mobile phone and called up the girl squirrel who he'd made friends with on the football pitches. They'd bonded over teams and nut skills.

He went round to hers and they ate nuts and did kick ups and watched films and had so much fun Nuts didn't even notice 27 missed calls from a depressed Zoomer.

Hows that big man? Good story?
Big man?

My anger is second hand.
You left me your temper and it kept me protected.

- Sshhh. You have to be quiet. They're asleep. Come on.

Tip toeing downstairs in the dark. Closing the living room door. seeing the video shop case. Knowing.
- Now here's the deal. You can't tell your mom, okay? There'll be shooting and killing in this and you know she doesn't like that kind of thing. Yes, and swearing. Probably lots. But your a big boy now, you can handle that can't you? Okay, so nobody knows. Our secret right? Deal?
His big hand.
Sitting next to him on the floor, leant against the sofa.
The ORION studios logo coming out of the stars. Magic.

Earlier that afternoon, looking up at it on the video shop shelf and him shaking his head.
- No way. Your mom would kill me.

I was 9.

I'd never seen anything anywhere near as violent in my life. The bit where they shoot him to bits made me cry, but I made sure to do it silently. Looking up at Dad from the corner of my

eye. When it was finished I pretended to be asleep so he'd have to carry me upstairs. That was the best bit.
When he closed my bedroom door, I just lay there staring at the ceiling. All I could see was Alex Murphy's body being shot to pieces.
Next day I was in the playground and Chris Northall wouldn't give me the ball or something and I called him a fucking bastard. I got a week outside the headmaster's office and a letter home. Mom found out about Dad showing me the film and they went at it. I remember lying at the top of the stairs, my chin on the rough carpet, listening to them shouting at each other, imagining Alex Murphy at the bottom of the stairs getting shot to pieces.

I remember looking at their wedding photographs. The panoramic shots with them two in the middle. On Mom's side, nearly a hundred people, family and friends all beaming. On Dad's side, his mom and dad, his brother and his best man. Four people.
The rest of his family refused to go because mom was mixed race. So he cut em off.
I always loved that. The conviction of it. The pride on his face. I want her.
I want her and if you're not fine with that you can fock off and never speak to me again.

You have to be able to sleep lad. Whatever happens, whatever you do,

you need to be able to shut your eyes and go. Only way you can do that is if you did what you wanted.
It's not always easy. There might be other people involved.
It doesn't matter. If you don't do what you want, you won't sleep. You'll lie there on your own. Next to someone. Knowing you ignored your gut. People'll always tell you to think. Think.
Like your head knows better than your gut. Let me tell you lad, at the end of the day your head doesn't know shit all next to your gut and the end of the day is when you have to sleep. You listen to your gut and do what you want. Cos if you can't sleep, you're no good to anyone.

FRIDAY

Eyes open.
Pain. Shooting behind my face into my skull.
All I can see is white. My lungs crushed.
Something squashing my throat.
I can here laughing. Blurred edges.
More voices. laughing.
I can't breath.
Your mom lifts your brother off my face and tells him that it's not fair to knee drop daddy when he's not awake yet.
You and him are in hysterics.
I can feel my blood
Ggggrrrrrrrrr-

Sometimes people are surprised. Genuinely.

- You're a dad? Really? But you're such a big kid.
Like what you're supposed to do is become a grown up fully first, then have children. Like you should wait until you've forgotten what's it's like to be one, before you have one.
Like our job is to teach our children to be grown ups.
Big kid?
I focking hope so

I finish painting the skirting board. The wet gloss catches the light. I roll onto my back and stare at the clean white ceiling.
I think about snow. I remember following Dad out to the garden wrapped up in a snow suit. Him leaving huge footprints as he made his way to the shed to get a shovel. I remember sitting in one of his footprints. Like a little car.
How could I have sat in his footprint? How big were his feet?
A paper bag full of pasty hits the floor an inch from my head.
I sit up.
Chris Moyles says something unfunny. Andy laughs and throws me something.
- What's this?
- If you don't know what it is you're kinda screwed, mate
The cover is hard and matt black. Inside the pages are thick sketchbook paper. I run my hand over the white page.
- No more scraps of bog roll or sandpaper yeah?
- Thank you

- Alright. It's just a book, don't try and bum me.

And we're laughing on our backs with mouths full of pasty.

I'm looking up at nan as we sit together on the sofa. She's telling me a story about a crafty spider tricking other animals out of their food. There's no book and I wonder how many stories she has in her head. The cords in her neck tighten as she speaks. She uses her hands a lot. And then what happened Nan?
Well, I think that's up to you.

Tarzan's Jane taps her phone with long nails.
- Glad you could come back. This could be big for you. Lets hope he thinks you're funny.
The back end of the fibre glass plane sticks out towards me. I think of the pilot. Squashed and bloody. Crushed into a mangled mess when the fake plane smashed into the wall.
When I was nineteen I had a dream that I had a tiger's head tattooed on my shoulder. I woke up in the middle of the night and sketched the tiger's face as I'd seen it.
In the morning I found the picture next to my bed and decided I had to have it tattooed onto me for real. I found a good place, chatted to the guy, he did a version of my sketch with thicker

lines and a week later I had the tiger's face on my left shoulder for life. Your mom didn't like it. She didn't get why I'd choose to mark my body forever. We argued.

I think about how you called it my tiger button when we went swimming and how we decided it was what I pressed when I needed extra strength to battle evil.

Jane hangs up her phone and looks for me. The deep leather sofa is empty. The massive fake fish stares out. It's rubber mouth carved into a smile.

It's not a steady build up. It's not more and more pebbles being added to the scale until it tips. It's not accumulation.
But it's not instinct.
It's not the body acting before the brain is engaged,
It's something else. It's staring consequence in the face and doing it anyway. Just like I was taught.

Chris Moyles starts to say something unfunny.
I switch the radio off. Whoever buys this house and moves in and sits watching telly on their deep leather sofa will never know that, just a couple of feet away, underneath a millimetre of paint, there's a picture me and Andy drew of a tiger in

a gorilla mask bumming a monkey.

I stare out of the window at the space where there was rubble and I think of a garden. Nothing grand. Big enough to kick a ball around. One on one, one goal and in. There's hedges on one side and a tree. A proper tree. Big enough to wanna climb. No need for a shed. It's mostly grass.

There's a bench, so you could just sit looking out and one of them little brick barbeques. I can knock one of them up. Close enough to the kitchen window to reach in for more burgers or a drink.

There's laughing. And you.

And you.

- Yo, where's my phone?

- That is nuts.

I was just gonna phone you. Right now. I swear down. I had the phone in my hand and you rang

Maybe. Look, I wanna say something

Can I go first please?

I wanna come. Move down. I wanna move down and I want us to find a place and move in and do it. I know what I said, but I mean it. Yes. I'm sure. If you still want me there I want to come. I want you.

There. Done. Your turn.

You're what? _____

The nurse handed you to me and all I could think was how light you were. How I was bracing my arms to feel the weight of a person and how it felt like I was cradling a balloon. I could feel the bones in my arms. I looked at your mom. Her eyes full of tired and tears. Strands of dark hair stuck to the edges of her face.

- You did this

I laid you on her chest and your little face moved up, nuzzling to her chin.

- Look what you did.

- Look what we did.

I remember thinking, this changes everything.

Nothing is going be the same.

I looked around. The mid wife, the nurses. The look on their faces. Then it hit me. Our moment is one of many. Everyone else in the room has been here before many times before.

They're looking at us like somebody else's children taking our first steps.

As I lower you gently into the weighing scales the short nurse tells me you're not made of glass. As she takes you off me and flips you round you start to cry. She's pulling off your towel like you're just another toy on a conveyer belt and every little part of me wants to punch her in the face.

My first ever gig I won £20 and a phone. It was a dark blue

Nokia, one with these orange strips down the sides. I was the last one of us to get one. I made Andy come with me.
We sat in the pub around the corner before it started and got merry on Jack Daniels.
We spent the £20 on a Chinese and sat on the Bullring steps.
I remember Andy burning his mouth on his pancake roll and us laughing and him saying.
- You should do more of this

I know that there's people above us.
Past the glass and the metal. Past the layers of concrete and earth and girders and dirt. I know they're there. Crossing the road.
Smoking outside.
Talking. Thinking. Making decisions.
I stare at my dark reflection in the tube train window. The lines in my forehead are deep and there are circles under my eyes. I think about how you said that this is when we age.
These nights of no real sleep and days that don't belong to us. This is when we age. Orbiting around little lives, carrying our dreams in ruc sacs, we don't notice.
We brush our teeth in the same mirror and one morning we catch our own eye and realise we look how old we are.
Our faces caught up with our birthdays.
And it's fine, you said. That's the way it works.

The only people unhappy with it, the ones clinging onto what they can't get back are the ones who haven't accepted it, and the only reason you can't accept it is because you don't know what you want.

In a few minutes this train will reach a station and I'll get off, ride up an escalator on the right hand side and emerge where we live.

I'll walk down the street we chose without planning and I'll look up at the front door to our flat. The flat we scrape to afford and I'll turn my key in the door in slow motion because you'll be asleep. I'll tred on the edges of the stairs as I climb and manoeuvre myself over the child gate in silence.

I'll leave the bathroom light off and I'll avoid the water as I pee and take my bag off, making sure you don't stir, and I'll go into the boys room.

I'll lift the duvet up over the shoulders of the one who gets cold and pull the duvet down on the one who always gets too hot and I'll pick up the Toy Story night light and go into our tiny kitchen.

I'll sit at our little table and pour four fingers of rum into a mug we bought in France and I'll stare at Buzz lightyears glowing face and I'll think about what we have. How much what we have revolves around what we do.

How what I do now is a million miles away from anything I ever thought I'd do. What I do didn't even exist.

And how at any point it could all stop.

Just like that.

If I'm not willing to tread a path that is laid out, and that some people would kill to tread, then at some point, chances are, I'm going to exhaust my options. I'm going to piss off the wrong person and doors that are currently on the latch will get pushed shut and padlocked and that will be that. Done.
My ideas won't matter. The space I've carved will be filled by someone else willing to play along and everything I've built will unravel to shit and I'll just be stuck outside in the rain with a salmon in my beard like Dan Akroyd in Trading Places.

But fuck me.

It'll be my fault.

end.

Thank you;

Bearwood, Cape Hill, Handsworth, Dudley Road Hospital, West Smethwick Park, Warley Woods, 42's, Halesowen College, Hagley Road, Erdington, Langley, Lightwoods Park, Neelam's, Sandro's 'save the horses' Ford Fiesta, Woolworths strawberry fizzy laces, orange chips, Karachi, The Chocolate Box, The VG, The ford cortina that knocked me down, The Bluebell Cafe, Greyhound Video, Sony discman, Rowley Regis, The Village Society, Digbeth, Quinton, The Wernley bartender who saved my hand, Harry Parkes, Dutchpot, Ladywood, The Rag Market, Red Fiery Dragon, Devil's Drop, Octopussy, Albright & Wilson, St Gregory's Primary, Strawberry Nourishment, Chester Castle, Rackham's 6th Floor cafe, Gillott Road, Dudley Tesco 24 Hour, Eat Wise, Harry Mitchell's, Hadley Stadium, Perryfields High, King's Cinema, The EDC, Edgbaston Reservoir, Adidas Kick, Cost Price, Preedy, Bearwood Sports, The extension, The Dog, The Abbey, Drogheda, Monk Bretton, The Bear Hotel, The Duck, The Barclay Road fight, The Metrodome, Nostalgia & Comics, Swordfish Records, Mo Bay, Oasis Market, Medicine Bar, Intercity 125, Dusty, The Rainbow, Bullring Steps, Mango Rubicon, Poppy Red, The Glee Club, Mr Egg, Laurel Road Community Centre, Safebury's, Burntwood, The Steering Wheel, Fantex, Granddad big hands, LSD, The Nightingale, The 140, The 241, Birmingham REP, The mac, Thimblemill Library, Thimblemill REC, Thimblemill Baths and 184 Park Road.

I am where I'm from. Lucky, lucky boy.